CW01648340

Shifting Lines

epubli

Text copyright © 2021 by Annina Lux and VOICE writers
Published by Annina Lux, Project VOICE – Projecting Voices e.V.
Post Box 31 10 52, 10640 Berlin, Germany
(mail to: info@projectingvoices.org)

Cover image: Salar de Uyuni, Bolivian Salt Desert © Annina Lux

Printed by epubli – a service of neopubli GmbH, Berlin, 2021

Shifting Lines

Ten voices of change-makers working in their native country or region

Edited by Annina Lux

With the VOICE Team:
Florian Wintermeyer
Catherine Banner
Jonas Lux
Sheila Chepkoech
Alena Gold
Alexander Punter
Bárbara del Bosque Salmerón
Philina Tempelmeier
Margot Ossola
Jan-Frederik Westedt

Contents

Preface

Annina Lux

A line is a powerful thing. Drawn as a border, it can divide us. Used to join two points, it can connect us. Joined up in letters, it can tell a story. The story of VOICE is essentially one about lines.

The first of these lines came in the form of a warning. VOICE was founded in 2016 to project the voices of individuals working or volunteering in social, humanitarian and peace-related fields in their native country or region. Since the motivation for establishing VOICE came from my experience of returning to Europe after working in a rural hospital in Bolivia, naturally our first writer was Bolivian. But I am unable to name this writer precisely because of this line. When I first discussed the idea of sharing her story in our first book, *A Definition of Snow*, published in 2019, her response was instantaneous: Of course she would share her story; it needed to be heard. "But you know," she added, "this is crossing the line." By this, Chamuela (as she decided to call herself), meant that what she had to say was not what was deemed to be inside the acceptable perimeter line for voicing opinions by the Bolivian government. The fact that she was honestly sharing her experiences and thoughts about the challenges of working in a rural hospital put her at great risk of political, economic and social consequences for herself and her family. Nevertheless, she crossed that line without hesitation – because she wanted to change the situation, as she explains in her story.

Since then, VOICE and its writers have been crossing lines many times. By breaking the silence about what is too often not spoken about. By going against "official" opinions. By brushing aside dominant stereotypes. By standing up for what they believe in. By courageously sharing their own experiences, challenges and dreams – irrespective of what they are expected to say and do. In doing so, they also constantly push this line a little further, changing the status quo for the better every time they step across. Shifting this line requires an enormous amount of bravery. It creates an equally enormous impact, one small step at a time.

The second of these lines emerged in the form of perimeters. For the launch of our first book, *A Definition of Snow,* our writer Golda wrote a speech, as an ambassador for the fourteen VOICE writers that shared their stories. The sentence that I remember most distinctly from the entire speech – printed in this book as "Notes from a VOICE writer" – is this one: "I didn't think I had anything to contribute to Project VOICE." I recall this because anyone who has met Golda will immediately tell you that nothing could be less true. And I recall it because it is a sentence I have heard from many of our writers. I can assure you that this has nothing to do with a lack of self-confidence or ability. Indeed, I believe there are few people with the strength, courage, passion and perseverance of these inspiring individuals. If anything, it goes to show their humility. Instead, I believe it is a result of perimeters drawn around us, geographically and culturally: ominous lines that, for many of our writers, block their voices from reaching beyond their own communities and circles. Such perimeters are, of course, not always a bad thing – delineating culture can help us to form a community and sense of belonging and identity. However, such perimeters also block our writers' voices from reaching beyond their traditional boundaries. After five years of working with VOICE, it still amazes me, again and again, just how hard it is for our writers to be heard outside their perimeter. And with how much power and perseverance each of our writers makes their story heard.

Such a perimeter line also surrounds our audiences. When I decided to work in a rural hospital in Bolivia, many of the people I spoke to about this were not able to place Bolivia on the correct continent. They could not name Bolivia's capital city. They did not know the official language(s) spoken there. This is not at all because they were uninterested or uneducated – on the contrary, this group included some of the smartest people I know, and all of them were incredibly interested in learning more about Bolivia before, during and after my time there. But Bolivia, a country far away from their homes, was simply out of reach for them. Outside of the perimeters drawn by geography (Europe) and culture ("The Western world"[1]). In the very periphery of education in their countries, and not in focus in the media, Bolivia was literally "out of bounds". In fact, this very perimeter was one of the reasons why we founded

[1] VOICE is aware of the controversial discussions surrounding terms such as 'the Western world' and 'Global North/South'. However, in line with our writers' use of these terms, we have decided to employ the most frequently used terminology.

VOICE, as explained in *A Definition of Snow*. By projecting our writers' voices and connecting our writers with our audiences, VOICE has redrawn and widened those perimeters for our writers and audiences, at least on a small scale. VOICE has shifted these individually enclosing lines to create a shared space, making our writers' powerful, honest and thought-provoking stories available to our audiences and enabling exchange.

The third line was unexpected but not altogether surprising – the individual connection formed within and between the members of the VOICE team, the VOICE writers and the readers. When I founded VOICE in 2016, it was essentially in response to the unavailability of voices like those of my Bolivian colleagues to Western audiences. But this experience, it turned out, was not just my own, but mirrored by many of those people I am lucky to count as my friends, many of whom are now part of VOICE. We wanted to open up a space for our VOICE writers to share their experiences and thoughts, previously unheard by Western audiences. To project their voices beyond perimeter lines. What I did not realize at the time, however, is that the nature and impact of VOICE went far beyond telling the stories of our inspiring VOICE writers.

When I came back from a remote rural setting in Bolivia, it was odd to adjust to the easily available experiences of urban life in Germany. One of these experiences was going out for dinner. Wanting to see friends and family after the eight months I was gone, dinner meetings were numerous. After eight months of mostly eating different combinations of pasta, rice, potato, tomato and chicken, it was of course nice (if odd, not being used to it any more) to enjoy some different food. However, spending double the daily wage of the average Bolivian family in the town I worked in (roughly seven euros) was not. It kept me thinking, and it made me feel highly uncomfortable. I kept calculating just how many vaccines my dinner expenses could buy, how much gauze we would have been able to purchase, how much medication it would have delivered. When I shared this thought, I was often told in a comforting tone that I wasn't to worry, *this* would normalize again, with time. The comment was meant well, of course, and I am grateful for the support. But in my mind, I was sure that they had brutally mixed up the subject of the sentence, *this* referring to me being uncomfortable at the disparity between my life and that of my Bolivian colleagues just a week after having said good-bye to them. In fact, the problem was my former Bolivian neighbours having to house, feed and clothe their families with half of the amount of money I was spending for one dinner. I carefully hinted at this, and they brushed it off in a well-meaning way saying that they, unfortunately, couldn't relate because they didn't have a connection to this other reality. None of them meant this in a mean or negative way at all. Nevertheless, I couldn't help but feel disconnected.

As VOICE grew, many of our team, writers and readers shared this feeling. At the book launch of *A Definition of Snow*, one of my friends came up to me and said: "Now I understand what you meant." The same sentiment was mirrored in many of the messages we received, some of which were addressed to individual writers, sharing how the reader related to their individual story. One of our readers wrote: "Every life tells a story, and bringing so many stories together brings lives together." What a perfect summary. Suddenly, our readers could relate to our writers, and interact with them. This meant the world to us at VOICE – VOICE had managed to shift the lines between our writers, our team and our readers from borders into connections.

The very last of these lines actually speak for themselves – the lines forming our writers' stories. These lines hold the potential to change the narrative. It takes courage and dedication to cross a line. It also takes courage to share your story. Very few of our VOICE writers write professionally, and for some this was the first or longest story they had ever written. Each of our VOICE writers uses these lines differently, weaving them into powerful individual testimonies, or employing them to paint pictures of unfailing dedication and passion for making an impact. The most constant advice I have received from people over the years is that individuals cannot save the world. I have always believed this was wrong. In fact, I think *Shifting Lines* is yet again proof that individuals can change the world – each of the ten writers in this book do just that, on a daily basis, alongside millions of change-makers across the world. In 2019, our regional coordinator and VOICE writer Sheila Chepkoech and I went to visit the home for disabled children in Nairobi she wrote about in her story. When we greeted the kids, one of them started laughing and hugging Sheila as she said hello. It was Mark[2], who clearly recognized

[2] To protect the identity of the child, his name was changed.

her. His pure joy at seeing Sheila was, to me, the best proof that it is possible to change someone's entire world.

Readers always ask me how I get to meet the inspiring individuals that become our VOICE writers. The answer is actually pretty simple. They are the people who go where everyone else is leaving. Who stand up when everyone else is sitting down. Who speak up when everyone else is silent. Who reach out when all others are looking away. Who look for answers when everyone else is asking questions. Who move when everyone else is waiting. They are the people you meet when you move not just one, but ten extra miles beyond the point of requirement. *Shifting Lines* brings together ten such individuals. Whether their story is about standing up, speaking up, reaching out, asking questions or acting – their stories are powerful, thought-provoking and inspiring. And, individually as well as collectively, they are shifting lines.

VOICE is about the shifting of lines. The shifting of those lines our writers cross on a daily basis to change the status quo. The shifting of the lines delineating perimeters that keep us apart. The shifting of lines drawn as a border to lines drawn as a connection. And the shifting of lines into stories that change the narrative. We invite you to join us in *Shifting Lines*.

Annina is the founder and head of VOICE and the editor of Shifting Lines *and also of* A Definition of Snow, *the first anthology of VOICE writers published in 2019.*

Notes from a VOICE Writer

Golda Poni

When I was contacted by my good friend Sheila Chepkoech, VOICE's Regional Coordinator for Africa, about contributing my voice to a book that aimed at sharing the different experiences and perspectives of humanitarian workers across the world, I was working in my small home county of Kajo-Keji in South Sudan with a Christian organization called CRESS. CRESS focused on child sponsorship and women's empowerment through small businesses, agriculture, and savings. To be very honest, I had just completed university and was trying to navigate what the future held for me in terms of my career – and I didn't think I had anything to contribute to VOICE. But Sheila encouraged me, telling me that the work we did was quite amazing and was worth sharing – so I decided to give it a shot.

Contributing to VOICE over the next couple of months took me on a personal journey of introspection into my own contribution to humanitarian work, and an intentional examination of what my work and that of many others actually meant for those we served. I asked myself the difficult questions and those questions in turn laid bare the impact on our beneficiaries of the work we did. In the beginning, it might have seemed like it was me who had something to offer VOICE but, as I finished writing my piece for the project, I realized that I had been given so much more than I could ever imagine, in the form of many valuable lessons that have stuck with me to this day. In light of the publication of *Shifting Lines*, I thought I would share some of the lessons I drew from writing for VOICE in *A Definition of Snow*, because we all have a role to play in our various fields, and the work we do does have a certain impact on those who benefit from it.

1. There is power in your voice. Your voice reveals the unseen and is the foundation for the confidence, freedom, hope, and future of those you serve. So don't hide your voice because it can affect someone's breakthrough, transformation, and future.

2. As humanitarian workers, our role goes beyond our job descriptions. Our duty is fundamentally to the human beings we serve and in order to fully undertake this role, our work must be preceded by our ability to be and stay human in the most consistent manner possible.

3. More often than not, it's not about what you can offer but what those you serve are willing to receive. Even though their livelihood may entirely depend on the services we have to offer, they deserve to have a choice. They deserve to determine what works best for them because, in the end, that's the only way our work will remain impactful and sustainable. More importantly, it's the only way we can empower them and break the vicious dependency cycle that is such a challenge in humanitarian work. So we must always remember that it's not about us, but about them.

Today, I continue to be involved in humanitarian work in Northern Uganda with South Sudanese refugees and local Ugandan communities as a Monitoring and

Evaluation Manager, and yet three years down the road, the lessons I drew from the time I contributed my voice to *A Definition of Snow* continue to guide, motivate, and inspire me in my work – to make a more meaningful contribution to humanity.

Just like *A Definition of Snow*, *Shifting Lines* is more than a book, it is a union of voices calling out for responsibility, positive change, humanity, sustainability, and ultimately, a better world for everyone!

Golda is a VOICE writer who shared her story in our last book, A Definition of Snow, *published in 2019.*

Do Not Aid – Serve: Lessons from the Chiquitano forest

Jhanisse Vaca Daza (Bolivia)

I was nineteen years old when I met David. He was nine. I still remember that warm afternoon in Santa Cruz, Bolivia, when I walked into his hospital room and his big brown eyes focused on me with curiosity. He was a patient in the hospital where I was volunteering. Like many children in our country, Bolivia, David had contracted HIV from his mom, who did not know she had it. This mother-to-child transmission of HIV could have been prevented with proper medical treatment, if my country had proper healthcare and better living conditions for its citizens. But it doesn't. And so David was sitting in front of me, in a hospital room, with his whole childhood interrupted by a disease caused by a virus he had been born with. Yet with time I have come to realize he was the healthiest, most wholesome soul I will ever meet.

David never thought of himself as a victim. In fact, if there is a real-life, flesh-and-bone hero in my life, it is him. He was the most joyful, funny, and energetic child I have met. As a hospital volunteer helping with feeding, bathing and supporting patients, I was at first more concerned with his physical needs. But he was quick to guide me to his real needs. David did not need doctors, or myself, to look at him as a "lesser" or "weaker" person because of his health condition. Our pity was not nourishing to him. The first step for us to really uplift him was to recognize his dignity. Like any other child, he just needed to be treated with respect, as the whole, complete human being he was, thinking and feeling and sometimes even laughing in front of us. And once he unknowingly taught me this, and our relationship became that of two equal friends supporting each other, I could see how even his physical health improved.

Initially, David did not want to eat hospital food. He felt guilty that he had free food in the hospital while his family, who lived on the streets, often did not have anything to eat. He would try to save his food, hidden and wrapped with napkins, so he could give it to his mom or siblings if and when they came to visit. This maturity and self-sacrifice in a nine-year-old is sadly common to many children in Bolivia whose families live in poverty. The doctors, his psychologist included, were quite worried about this behaviour and initially I was too. But in time, as I learned to "be" with him more than vertically trying to "make him" do things, I noticed he was more likely to eat if I also brought food and we ate together. So we would spend the morning painting, drawing, dancing and singing and right before leaving, I would have lunch with him while we listened to our favourite music. Seeing him eat was one of my favourite parts of the day, especially because I realized in those moments that I was not "helping him". We were helping and uplifting each other.

One thing that always struck me about David was how much he loved Bolivia. Despite having grown up on the streets, cleaning cars for coins and not attending school regularly, David had a strong sense of love and pride for the country that had failed him. I could not help but think that the country he loved so much and the red-yellow-and-green flag he often painted was one of the reasons why he was sick. I knew that had he been born in a different country he would have had better chances of having his HIV treated earlier on. But he had no resentment, no anger, towards the country that wronged him as a baby and the society that ignorantly feared and stigmatized him for having HIV as a child. Instead, he loved Bolivia deeply and talked about the little bits he knew of our history constantly. When his end was near, he made me promise I would continue to work for

Bolivia and for children like him. I swore I would. And today I am writing these lines to you, dear reader, in the hopes of keeping that promise alive.

Ever since meeting David, when I was finishing high school, I have been trying to understand how I can contribute with my work so that Bolivia can become a country that does not fail its children and its environment. It's still an evolving quest. I was able to gain scholarships to go to university and study International Relations in the USA, thinking, at that young age, that the power to change things was in the hands of powerful governments and international institutions. I thought if I could work in those entities, maybe I could use that power to do good. It did not take too much time to realize these ideas were wrong. I then tried to work in every other area that I thought could "make a difference": Volunteering in NGOs with high, noble missions like UNICEF, running around authorities with political journalists in Bolivia, working with institutions that support child victims of sexual abuse in public schools, volunteering for environmental causes, and then back to working in international NGOs that advocate for justice globally. Of course, all of these initiatives bring much needed immediate support to people who would not otherwise get it – but they don't solve the root problems that cause these injustices. All of the above come short of bringing the real "change" that so many Western institutions promise, for the same reason that I initially failed to understand my hero-child in that hospital room over a decade ago.

To many people in the Western world, "developing"

nations are like a sick child sitting in a hospital bed in front of them. You look at us and talk about us in a paternalistic tone, as if we weren't even aware of how bad we have it. You come into our room, into our territories, with the set expectation of "helping us", always you a step above us, always you trying to bring the solutions, always you coming to teach us about the unjust structures that once again you, that ever self-centring you, have created around the globe and trapped us with. Sometimes you even come with self-deprecation and anger towards your own governments, and you try to wash it away by washing our wounds, without really listening to what it is that is hurting us and opening *our* wounds to begin with. You come with aid programmes thought of in other countries, in other languages, in other realities, and feel that because you taught someone here to fish, you have saved the river, that because you carried out one successful fundraiser for someone who looks different to you, you have emancipated yourself from the Western guilt that you carry. But it doesn't work like that. You cannot keep pretending that you can separate the individual from their environment. You can't pretend to want to "save" or "help" my country if you don't understand the entirety of it and the entirety of yourself and your role in it as well. Your intentions may be pure, and I thank you and I honour them, but we cannot be tools to solve your own societal issues. You have to respect us as well.

I am here to tell you, lovingly, what David taught me with his life and untimely death: Bolivia does not need your pity, Bolivia needs you to know who we are before you act in our reality. Like many other "developing" nations, my country was born to independence, in 1825, with a societal structure that still neglected and abused indigenous communities and Afro-descendants. The harmful social norms and practices inherited from the Spanish colony did not end when our independence was proclaimed. You might know this from your history lessons. The structure of our modern "state" was built around the interests of the elites at the time, hence this nation-state was not built, as it should have been, in unity with all those who inhabit Bolivia. This led to a state with a real presence and capacity only in areas that were considered relevant for the elites, and subsequently to governments that still today respond only to those interests – the face and last names of people who compose those elites may have changed with time, but the structures and corruption that sustain them remain in place.

Likewise, the experience of being "Bolivian" is widely different for people in my country depending on the geographical region, ethnicity, and socio-economic level we live in. Our societal divides – already existent from our many indigenous nations and regions forced together during colonialism and our republican history – are made even deeper by our drastically different experiences with the state – or more often than not, its absence. And, while this plurality is even greater than I can explain today, much Western analysis – whether it be from academics, journalists, NGOs or even governments – tries to reduce it to a dualistic battle that responds far more to the dualistic (and therefore individualistic) dilemmas and lenses of Western societies than to Bolivia's lived reality. That's why I say: you can't pretend to help us if you don't even know us. You have to understand the environment in which we live if you want to bring constructive action to it.

The weakness of the Bolivian state is one of the main reasons why, no matter how much international aid pours in, we still can't stand on our own. When I talk about the state's "weakness" I do not only refer to its physical absence in many regions of our country, but to the weaknesses of its institutions and their capacities as well. It is no secret that in my country the executive, legislative and judicial branches lack independence and are often instrumentalized by political parties in power. This has been acknowledged by those who have studied my country deeply, such as the academic Laurence Whitehead, who deemed Bolivia one of the countries of the world most plagued with "endemic crises of authority". Likewise, we have one of the worst justice systems in the world, which has also been acknowledged by international institutions such as Freedom House and World Justice Project. This last organization conducts its analysis based on the perception of each country's inhabitants themselves, and Bolivian responses to their polls ranked Bolivia as one of the seven worst jurisdictions in the world. Transparency International also conducts polls with locals and their 2019 Corruption Perception Index ranks Bolivia in the 123rd place out of 180 countries in terms of corruption. It is not that the Bolivian people lack confidence in their government and state, it's that the state never did and still has not provided actions to earn their confidence or respect in the first place.

If the state, then, is neither present nor efficient in every area of the country, or even trying to be, how valuable are the rules it supposedly abides by? I have found that most foreign institutions working in Bolivia, whether diplomatic missions, international bodies or aid-providing NGOs, analyse our country with the same lenses that they analyse their own. They believe that because our constitution is the first one in the world to grant rights to Mother Earth or because our government officials pronounce eloquent speeches in the UN, then we must be doing OK. They fail to realize that local leaders easily take advantage of the Western world's obsession with legislative texts, symbolic scriptures and words, to disguise the reality of government abuse and corruption on the ground.

Foreign entities and their workers, who have made the conscious choice of travelling to and working in a different country, must take it upon themselves to learn about these deceptions and factor them into their own analysis. Believing that problems in countries like mine are solved with the creation of new laws or have been solved by them is assuming that the Bolivian state works exactly like a Western one. Believing that channelling all "aid" and "cooperation" through the Bolivian state will lead to this aid reaching people in need and will not be another source for local corruption is also delusional, even if it is uncomfortable to acknowledge. This too is colonialist thinking and deeply harmful. If foreign institutions come into Bolivia – as they do – with an analysis made from a purely Western perspective and without listening to civil society on the ground, these institutions' plans and actions will be based on such an analysis and, therefore, never truly contribute to Bolivians' lived experiences. And here lies the key to real, constructive action: civil society.

The truth of a state's efficiency can only be measured by the checks and balances carried out by civil society. This is the whole basis of Locke's social contract. In countries like Bolivia, where state institutions are weak and rule of law is barely existent, the role of civil society is all the more important. Throughout Bolivia's history, the inefficiency of the state has often left empty spaces that have been occupied by labour unions, cooperatives, collectives, and other sorts of civil organizations. Social movements have played a determining role in our identity and history despite the many and brutal challenges they have faced when expressing their demands. Bolivian civil society, outside of political parties and government institutions, is a key and central actor of Bolivia's political environment.

This understanding is what led me to drop all previous aspirations of governmental and international work and focus on building a nonviolent grassroots movement in Bolivia. I have found in nonviolence as a sociopolitical technique the answers I could not find in any other branch of political science and general academia. The fundamental solutions to problems in countries like mine must come from the people themselves, but this cliché phrase means nothing if said people don't have the skills and tools to demand and/or propose those solutions to rigid and often authoritarian government structures. Nonviolence strategies and tactics, as explained by authors such as Gene Sharp and Srdja Popovic, provide the ordinary citizen with the tools to self-organize, mobilize, expose injustices, and pressure the state to acknowledge and solve them. This is the only type of action that, paired with education and unity campaigns, can lead to long-lasting results – which has been proven scientifically. Studies conducted by political scientists Erica Chenoweth and Maria J. Stephan have shown that nonviolent campaigns are successful in creating sustainable change 56 per cent of the time, twice as much as violent ones, which are common in countries with high amounts of inequality.

The deep study of nonviolence led a group of friends and I to found Ríos de Pie ("Standing Rivers" in English) in Bolivia in 2018. We were worried about the political and social conflicts in our country and hoped to give young people an alternative form of protest that did not resort to violence but empowered the citizenry instead. Ríos de Pie is now a youth movement focused on defending human rights and the environment in Bolivia, through nonviolent action and strategies. We want a free, fair and safe Bolivia that respects indigenous rights and has environmentally sustainable policies. We have been able to create a small yet united team of people from many different regions and backgrounds in Bolivia and we work through both service to our communities during crises as well as through political protests demanding government reform. We are still a small and relatively new group in comparison to many other Bolivian civil society groups, but we have been able to learn from indigenous leaders and human rights defenders who have been doing this work for much longer than us. Pairing this transmitted knowledge with innovative and creative protests has allowed us to become a recognizable actor in local issues. Likewise, we have also provided practical help during several environmental or social crises, teaming up with other citizens' groups. Our experience so far has taught us of Bolivians' high capacity to organize and support each other's communities outside of governmental channels.

Yet Bolivian civil-society groups are the last ones to be heard or supported by international bodies. Most Western institutions speak only to and cooperate with the Bolivian state, unknowingly (or let's hope so) providing even more resources for the corruption, abuse and centralization of power executed by the government at all its levels. Meanwhile, in the crises that Bolivian people have experienced in the last years, it has often been their own work – outside of the state and government – that has helped them out of despair. Allow me to illustrate better with two examples, one of civil society responding to devastating forest fires and another one about COVID-19 pandemic response.

Bolivia experienced its biggest environmental crisis to date in 2019-2020, when wildfires consumed millions of hectares in the eastern part of our country. The Chiquitano forest in Bolivia is one of the world's largest and most important tropical dry forests, with plants and animals uniquely adapted to this climate and soil. It is part of the Amazon basin, and the hills and mountains of this region are fundamental for supplying water to the Pantanal, the world's largest tropical wetlands. Despite its global importance, in the last two years Bolivia has lost over 10 million hectares of this region to government-encouraged fires. Over 6 million animals have died, 400 indigenous communities have been affected, and it is unknown how much damage there is to indigenous uncontacted communities within the forests. It is important to note that these forests were home to Ayoreo indigenous communities in the Ñembi Guasu and Kaa Iya area, the only uncontacted indigenous community in Latin America outside Amazonia.

In the years leading to this tragedy, the Bolivian government had enacted more than ten laws and executive orders that encouraged burning in order to expand the agricultural frontier. It is important to note that this expansion is for both beef and soya production for export to countries like China, not for feeding the Bolivian people. The government even approved a kind of forgiveness for fines for illegal burning in the middle of the fire season, enacted as Law 1171. All these actions by the Bolivian government have been categorized as ecocide by the International Rights of Nature Tribunal (2020)[3]. In their ruling after a careful assessment of the 2019 fires, the IRNT stated, "The promulgation and enforcement of laws and administrative policies which condoned burning in order to expand the agricultural frontier and which guaranteed impunity for illegal burning, as well as the weak institutional framework of the state bodies at their different levels of government responsible for the control and supervision of forests, have been fundamental factors in causing events denounced in this case."

---

[3] An international group which aims to create a forum for people from around the world to speak on behalf of nature.

Governmental response to the fires was equally detrimental. Despite the demands of communities displaced by the fires, firefighters and first responders, the central government refused to declare a national emergency in 2019. There were protests in at least five cities demanding the national emergency declaration, but central government authorities refused to act. This also meant that no firefighting equipment and/or donations for the firefighter teams could enter the country, since this is only permitted when a national emergency is declared. The Bolivian government also threatened journalists and activists who dared to denounce these obstructions to firefighting efforts. I was one of the activists who spoke to the international press about the fires and was consequently threatened with death by government supporters during this time. The Committee to Protect Journalists published a report about the highly dangerous environment during the fires for environmental reporters, in which a local journalist mentioned the government's threats to withhold state advertising from critical news outlets and filing lawsuits against critical reporters.

Despite these difficulties, civil society effectively mobilized and delivered over forty tons of equipment, food and medicines for firefighters through informal civil society networks only. Ríos de Pie, along with other environmental groups, managed to create a network of neighbourhood donation sites in five cities of Bolivia and, in cooperation with local airlines, we transported these donations to the fire areas. We also coordinated with more than twelve firefighter units and mobilized one ton of supplies during the 2020 fires. Given the informality of these civil efforts there are no official measurements of the total amount of aid delivered among all citizen groups. There are also no official institutions that can make it their task to do the corresponding investigation and documentation efforts. This is one space where NGO or other academic efforts could be useful, but there are no actors offering such support to civil society currently.

Another even more mesmerizing achievement of civil society in this region came as a response to the COVID-19 pandemic. In the little town of Santiago de Chiquitos in the east of Santa Cruz (the same region where forest fires took place in 2020), civil society took it upon themselves to build a hospital when the pandemic began. This small community, with no more than 2,500 inhabitants, capitalized on their previous experience with self-organization during the 2019 fire crises. The same citizens who led the Local Emergency Committee (COEL in Spanish) then, began organization in the town to prevent COVID-19 spread as the entire country entered a lockdown in March 2020. They included municipal authorities in the COEL, but also non-governmental ones such as water cooperatives, neighbourhood councils, business owners and local volunteers, among others.

Through this organization led by civil society, Santiago de Chiquitos managed to regulate entry and departure of people from the town, provide first responders with personal protective equipment, provide meals for families affected by the lockdown, and provide transportation to acquire food and medicines from other towns throughout 2020. While the municipality and military personnel collaborated with the efforts, the leadership and operational efforts came from non-state actors. Once all of these operations were set in place, they proceeded with the real challenge: How to put together a physical space where the town's doctors could effectively quarantine and treat COVID patients.

Yuvinka Gareca, neighbourhood leader and part of the COEL, told me about the organization that took place in order to fit out a new health building. The town leaders decided to re-build an abandoned hospital whose construction by the central government began in 1977 but was never properly finished. Many walls and ceilings had collapsed in the construction and there were even trees growing up inside the structure. Yuvinka said that the construction planning and work was carried out thanks to the pro-bono service of a retired architect, Mary Pacheco, who, along with the town's own people, executed the construction.

The initial 1970s construction had a main wing in the front and four "modules" or smaller structures around it, all of these abandoned. In order to finish the building quickly, the town divided the modules between each of their neighbourhoods by drawing lots. This allowed for both decentralized execution of the building work as well as for each neighbourhood taking ownership of their work. The people themselves agreed to work so that each module would have two rooms and a private bathroom. Military men from a nearby station also volunteered, helping with cleaning of the construction area. They coordinated with the townspeople to do this on days when no one from the town was working in construction, to minimize the risk of COVID contagion.

Most of the construction work was finished by October, when COVID-19 was reaching rural areas along with the beginning of the second wave in Bolivia. As reports of this town-made hospital reached local news in Santa Cruz, more civil society organizations, families and individuals contributed with donations of equipment and money – sometimes even coming from Bolivians abroad. Some of the donations received were washing machines, freezers, toilets, disinfection equipment, hospital beds, roof and floor tiles, among other things. The coordination for transport of these donations was also done by volunteers. Once the work was completed, local authorities formally requested regional governorship for funds to hire a medical doctor to work in this town. The governorship complied with this request. The people of Santiago de Chiquitos and their exceptional leadership building and refurbishing their own health centre in 2020 is perhaps one of the best incarnations of a national motto: Unity is strength.

While these two examples with which we at Ríos de Pie had personal experience are wonderful to illustrate the power of Bolivia's civil society, they do not represent the full extent of such capacity. Much solidarity work in Bolivia is done outside formal channels, and the lack of documentation and information to provide evidence of it is detrimental, in that Bolivian people are not even aware of their own strength. In a country with so many social divides and such low self-concept, this lack of knowledge of its positive values and capacities is a constant. This is one space where the support and action of foreign actors documenting and analysing civil society's capability – without interfering with it – could prove valuable. I think it's worth repeating: Solutions to Bolivians' problems must come from Bolivians ourselves, working in unity and building our strengths with solidarity, not as passive recipients of foreign "aid".

This knowledge of ourselves and our capacities as Bolivians is also fundamental to bringing the reforms needed to end corruption within the state. Power does not give up power voluntarily; state institutions will not resort to eliminating their own corrupt practices unless they are forced to do so by all of us who are victims of their abuse. Since international institutions value "sovereignty" above basic rights, they will never be the ones demanding this change inside corrupt or undemocratic states – and that position, while disappointing, is already known to us recipients of "international assistance". However, they could and should at the least redirect their eager will to "help" by providing opportunities for citizen empowerment in these societies. Spaces where citizens can reflect on their own historical experiences with nonviolent resistance and their current capacities to exert nonviolent campaigns should be at the forefront of any international "aid" efforts that hope to bring real, lasting change in any country. As Gandhi himself said in 1925: "Real independence will come not by the acquisition of authority by a few … but by educating the masses to a sense of their capacity to regulate and control authority."

The idea of foreign "aid" for my country should be based on a sense of voluntary interdependence among countries, not a vertical, pitiful handout that fortifies the abuser and creates a never-ending loop of dependence. Bolivia will never be able to stand on her own and contribute to the wider world to her fullest until her citizens are able to stand on their own and collaborate within their community. This cannot happen under state and government structures that profit from the crises of their people and the misdirected "aid" of foreign institutions. It also cannot happen while international bodies continue to remain timid in supporting demands for justice made by civil society while acting boldly on their unwitting contribution to economic gain within corrupt governments. While acknowledging the crimes inside their counterparts' structures may be uncomfortable and outside of diplomatic guidelines for international representatives, being accomplices to perpetual injustice and strengthening the abuser government's capacities should be even more embarrassing in its deviation from their proclaimed guiding values. The same can be said of assistance NGOs who focus on the wound but not the entirety of the patient, staying silent in front of injustice that they would not normalize or permit in their own countries. We should not have to continue bearing the consequences of foreigners' lack of moral courage.

You see, if David had lived (he would be 20 today), I would have wanted him to be the strongest and happiest young adult on this planet. I would have wanted to support him at his low points but above all to celebrate his achievements with pride. I would have wanted him to feel respected and accepted as an equal by society, to see his ideas validated and his work valued fairly. And above all, I would have wanted him to be independent and self-sufficient enough so that compassion and solidarity came naturally to him, not from a place of ego but from a place of understanding the interdependence among us all. That too is what I want for Bolivia. That too is how I hope you see us, before you try to hold our hand.

Just Making the Best Out of It: Life in a state of persistent crisis

Mercy Adong (Uganda)

My Personal Background

I was born in 1992 in the city of Gulu, Northern Uganda, which is close to the borders with South Sudan and the Democratic Republic of Congo. At that time and for many years afterwards, there was a fierce civil war in this area. The militias of a revolutionary but confused and brutal organization, calling itself the Lord's Resistance Army (LRA), devastated the north of Uganda, not only fighting against the government forces, but attacking mainly the rural population, torturing and killing many people, abducting others, and recruiting kids as child soldiers. In Gulu, the second biggest city in Uganda, which has a population of 150,000 today, a strong unit of government troops was stationed and so the rebels were never able to take this town. For the rural population it meant a safe harbour and each night people from the surrounding rural areas sought refuge there. Only recently has it come to my attention that this was captured in a film which is still accessible on the internet. It includes a video sequence of a song in German which dealt with the situation of kids coming to Gulu for shelter at night during the civil-war times. Although I don't understand the lyrics, watching the film took me back into the atmosphere of those days. The conditions in Gulu, which was flooded with destitute people, as well as in the nearby rural areas, were simply terrible and they determined the circumstances of my childhood and even later. Hunger and violence were commonplace.

However, the conditions in Uganda attracted the attention of the world and prompted many international aid organizations and foreign NGOs to get involved there, despite all the dangers, with Gulu as the centre. Without them, many more people would have died there than had already died anyway. These foreign supporters not only tried to feed the population, but above all the NGOs were and still are active in the social sector[4].

Not long after, my birth my family went back to my father's village, Lukodi[5], north of Gulu, even by bus a rather long drive via a bad dirt road. My father served as a policeman in Gulu during the week, and on weekends he returned to the family in Lukodi. Thinking about it now, I wonder how long it must have taken him, because he normally came by bicycle. However, when I was about three years old, my father left his family for another woman. He never paid alimony, so my mother, who until then had mainly been a housewife, had to support the family by whatever she could. In particular, ever since then and up to now whenever circumstances allowed she has tried to work by doing small-scale selling of foodstuffs at the markets. But the people had hardly any money to buy anything and we often had to go to bed hungry.

The turmoil of the civil war affected us very much and we had to flee several times. One of my first memories ever – which is still very unclear – is that we, along with many others, were rushed into a military helicopter and taken somewhere safe. In 1999 my mother and her then five children, of whom I was the youngest, were interned in a camp for internal refugees (official name: internally displaced persons, IDPs) in Pabbo. Pabbo was her birthplace and is situated in the district of Amuru, about 25

---

[4] This includes construction and operation of rural health centres, distribution of contraceptives, education to help the fight against HIV/AIDS, promotion of education and training, empowerment of women and much more.

[5] A settlement with a village character, but whose population had grown to several thousand people due to the influx of refugees.

minutes by bus from Gulu. It was not until 2006 that we were ordered by the authorities to leave the camp and return to Lukodi. Pabbo was smaller than Lukodi and slightly further away from Gulu, but much more accessible because of better road connections. Part of the government's strategy for fighting the rebels was to concentrate most of the northern rural population in such camps, whether they wanted to – many had fled of their own accord – or not. The aim was to prevent the rebels from being able to freely move, using the rural infrastructure, from small village to village like a fish in the water, forcing the villagers to nourish them and to provide support in various ways. At one time up to 90 per cent of the Acholi people, which is the main tribe in northern Uganda, are said to have been living in camps like this.

I remember our camp at the outskirts of the village as being huge. A large area had been cleared and a great number of traditional round huts with thatched roofs had been built on it, but much closer to each other than was customary in the villages. This turned out to be a problem, because it was a regular occurrence that a hut caught fire because cooking was done on an open flame. This problem is well known also in normal villages in the countryside and so there is always some distance from one hut to the other. In the camp, however, it was very difficult to get the fire of a burning hut under control and so it spread and each time quite a number of huts burnt down.

The camp was so large that it was divided into four zones, marked A, B, C and D, each with its own staff under a zone head, elected by the inhabitants. I cannot give an exact number, but in any case many hundreds of people lived there. The border of the camp was marked, but there was no protective wall or even a strong fence. However, security was provided by a considerable garrison of soldiers in Pabbo. So a camp like that gave the residents protection, to a certain extent. Some still wondered how effective this protection would be if a really serious attack by the rebels took place. I remember a joke that was told at those times. It ran as follows: the rebels are all hiding up in the mountains, where there are swarms of aggressive wild bees. The rebels therefore always have enough to do defending themselves against these bees and have no energy to come down to attack us. But we were lucky that Pabbo was never attacked.

Living very close together under these conditions led to the spread of infectious diseases in the numerous camps, such as malaria, typhoid fever and HIV, which in combination with the general shortage situation cost many thousands of lives, as we now know. We at that time were aware of many cases in our own camp, but didn't get figures about it.

The social life was also strongly influenced by living in the camp: the people who were crammed together here mostly came from manageable village communities, in which diverse interrelated family relationships existed and everyone knew everyone. There had been plenty of space, it was easy to meet for common activities if one wanted to or one could stay alone. Conflicts were solved within the community in accordance with traditional rules, providing special authority to the village elders. Now, however, everyone lived very close to previously unknown people, they could not avoid each other and the usual rules of living together lost much of their validity. The tone among children and adolescents was rough, fights over rank and the formation of rival groups were typical manifestations of this critical change. The weak were easily marginalized and badly treated. I myself did not want to be weak. Although I was not aggressive, I learned to defend myself against unfriendly children or adolescents and to assert myself, if necessary physically, against boys as well as girls. But more importantly, it was not difficult for me to make friends and, through their support, to have a counterweight to other, aggressive groups.

As far as nourishment is concerned, the basic supply was ensured by deliveries of food from the stores of the United Nations World Food Programme (WFP). Normally that worked well and the rations were, although small, sufficient to survive. But sometimes the food distribution was delayed which nearly immediately caused hunger. Anyhow, what we got was always limited to corn and beans, day in day out. And this food had often been in storage for a long time, so that the quality was low. In order to have ingredients for a more balanced diet, the inhabitants of the camp were on their own. Many of the families were therefore looking for opportunities to do some farming themselves in order to supplement the provisions that came from outside. Some tried their luck in micro-farming.

We were lucky that my grandmother had always lived in Pabbo, so she knew her way around. With her support, my mother was able to lease a small plot of land of perhaps two acres (about 0.8 ha) on which we cultivated crops, including millet, sesame and beans, some for our own consumption, but also to barter for other goods or, sometimes, even for a little bit of money, mainly from refugees who lived in the camp without being registered and therefore could not participate in the WFP rations. The fact that we had something to offer kept us afloat.

Despite my young age – initially only seven years – it was necessary and therefore taken for granted that I, too, took part in the work on the land. I got a solid grounding in the knowledge of practical agriculture and an understanding for the way of life of the rural population. This, as well as my own experiences from the internment in the refugee camp, helped me a lot in my later life. In 2006, when the government felt that the area was sufficiently pacified, we were asked to leave the camp and move back to my father's village, Lukodi.

Civil War Strikes my Family

Even in the time before we could officially return, individual family members were able to make short visits from time to time to the part of the family that still lived in Lukodi. This was not primarily about my father, but about the whole family network of grandparents, various uncles and aunts etc. Why at that time many people were still living in this place instead of being asked to move completely to one of the internal refugee camps, I cannot say. Maybe it had to do with the fact that Lukodi was quite close to Gulu and because an armed militia, a vigilante group, had been established there to defend this relatively large village and this was considered sufficient.

During one of these visits – it was 2004 and I had just turned twelve years old – I witnessed rebels entering the village. The people there were already used to them. Normally the rebels were mainly interested in taking food from us. If you gave it to them without resistance, you were usually spared. But there was never a guarantee of that and, from time to time, individual people were killed or kidnapped without any concrete reason, or children might be abducted to become child soldiers. Women were sometimes raped. But all these things had happened, if I remember correctly, before the vigilante group was set up.

Perhaps this time its establishment had aroused the rebels' anger. It was also assumed that the rebels had informers in the village and therefore knew relatively well what was going on there. In any case, this time, the militiamen came in much larger numbers than we were used to. In view of the rebels' superior numbers, the members of the vigilante group fled after a very short resistance. And, apparently, the rebels had come with the intention of killing from the start. They fired, without thinking twice, at men, women and children, at anyone they could see, and they also used machetes and bayonets. They fired into the huts and set many of them on fire, so that there was no safe hiding place. When the shooting started, I quickly fled together with one of my elder sisters into the wide bushy environment that existed near our village. Anyone else who had a chance did the same.

My grandfather, who had also fled, was worried about the family members who were left behind and went back quickly when things seemed to have quieted down a bit. As the rest of us returned to the village the next day, we found him dead near the village. He had wounds from blows with a machete or from being stabbed with bayonets and had been shot at the end. Most of the dead in the village were found right away; I think it was about 60 people. They were buried in a mass grave, but we didn't want that for my grandfather and we buried him ourselves close to our family's hut. The bodies of quite a number of others were found at later times in the area around the village. Even more people survived wounded. Again others disappeared without leaving a trace; probably they had fled never to come back or had been abducted. An aunt of mine had been kidnapped in this raid, too, and was forced to carry loot for the rebels. Right at the beginning, she was coerced to throw her three-month-old baby girl into the bush because it disturbed the rebels. Thank God she later managed to escape and her baby was also found and rescued after one day, her body covered with insect bites, but otherwise OK. This little girl, who nearly perished at that time, has developed into a pretty young woman.

Today there is a small civil war museum in the village of Lukodi and a monument, on which the names of the people who were murdered at that time are written, among them my grandfather's.[7] Only as recently as May 2021, the man responsible for the Lukodi massacre,

[7] For a more detailed information on the massacre in Lukodi see https://justiceandreconciliation.com/wp-content/uploads/2011/04/JRP_FNXIII_Lukodi-Massacre.pdf. I found this report only after writing down these memories of my own, and I don't want to mix my story too much with details and views which are reported by others, so I left my text unchanged.

Dominic Ongwen, was sentenced to 25 years in prison. He himself had been forced to serve as a child soldier at the age of nine, but had later taken on more and more leadership roles in the LRA and had become responsible for many terrible things. His punishment was a great satisfaction for all of us who had been affected by the massacre. Around the same time that these atrocities happened, my maternal grandfather died, too: he was a regular soldier in the government forces. When they tracked a unit of the rebels into the territory of the Democratic Republic of Congo, a skirmish ensued in which he was killed. To this day, his widow, my grandmother, has not received one cent of compensation or pension and she lives in very poor conditions. I am currently in the process of making an effort with the relevant authorities, trying to achieve some financial support for her. Although it is now no longer bluntly denied that she may actually have a claim, up to now no money at all has been paid.

My Education

I spent the first three years of primary school in the school which was attached to the refugee camp in Pabbo. After that I went to a public primary school in Gulu, which was situated within the compound of the prison there. The school was supported by the foreign NGO Save the Children and was mainly to allow the children of the inmates and the prison staff to get some basic education, but there were also a few places for outsiders like me. Because the NGO I mentioned gave financial contributions, my mother did not have to pay school fees for me, which she could not have afforded. Parents from the poor population like us often have great problems with paying the school fees – which quite some time ago were *officially* abolished. But the reality is different. For the poor these fees are often a reason not to send their children to school, or to take them out after a very few years. The school had boarding facilities where I could stay. Most schools in Uganda have boarding facilities, due to the dispersed rural nature of the population. I was usually only at home during holidays or, occasionally, at weekends.

The school system in Uganda still up to today largely follows the British example[6]. I am not familiar with all the details, however I am afraid that the qualifications we obtain here may not always be recognized in the United Kingdom as equivalent to the qualifications of the same name there. But, at least under local conditions, I was a good student and, after successfully going through an entrance examination, I was given the opportunity at the age of 14 to switch to a secondary school that was supported by the same NGO.

My dream was to become a doctor one day and I also had a promise from the NGO that they would support me until I reached A level, which would have given me

---

[6] Pupils can transfer to secondary school after seven years of primary school and a subsequent examination. After four years there, you can sit an exam for the Uganda Certificate of Education (UCE), which after the old British model is called O level. This is the qualification with which I left school. After a further two years at secondary school, you may take the exam for the Uganda Advanced Certificate of Education (UACE), called A Level, which in principle allows you to enter university.

access to university education. But in 2009, the last year before the O level exam, my mother was diagnosed with cancer. She now stayed sick at home and, as she was very weak, I had to take care of her and the family. As a result, my performance in school deteriorated and my O level result, although I still passed easily, was not as good as my previous results.

Nevertheless, I was offered the chance to continue my schooling. However, for that I would have had to leave Gulu and live in a boarding school elsewhere. But my mother was dependent on my care and so I dropped out of school. At that time I didn't think much about the further consequences, because my self-evident duty towards the family was the most important thing for me. Only very gradually did I realize that in the long run I had lost the privileged opportunity to continue my education so that I could perhaps have taken up my hoped-for profession as a doctor. In the following year, I contributed to the upkeep of the family by taking on various kinds of informal work in addition to caring for my mother, such as helping out with the sale of food at the market.

Finally, my mother had an operation and gradually recovered. I would have liked to continue my school education, but we could not finance it. However, I received another offer, which did not fully meet my wishes, but at least gave me the opportunity to learn something extra. There was a wealthy local politician from the ruling party who was willing to finance the training of ten suitable school dropouts as nursery teachers – both women and men. I was suggested to him and he accepted me. I nevertheless hoped that one day I would have the opportunity to shift to my hoped-for higher school career.

Until then, for lack of alternatives, I did this two-year course for nursery teachers. It was not that bad after all, as I love children. I passed at the end, as did five others who had started at the same time as me. Four others – all female – had given up early – as far as I remember not because they were not qualified, but because they either became pregnant or their husbands didn't want them to continue.

Occupations and Dreams

I received the Certificate in Early Childhood Development (ECD) in December 2013. Nurseries (kindergarten) in Uganda are part of the school system and their staff are called nursery teachers. I was able to work as a kindergarten teacher at a combined nursery and primary school until the end of 2014. My monthly salary after completion of the education was 80,000 Ugandan shillings, which at that time probably amounted to about US$30. That was the usual payment in this profession. This money was not enough in any way. The school itself also got further and further into financial difficulties and I therefore lost my job in the end. That was in December 2014. Because of the poor payment in this profession, I did not look for the same kind of occupation elsewhere, but tried my luck in all kinds of unskilled, informal work, mainly utilizing my previous experience in informal small-scale trading.

Nevertheless, always in the back of my mind I preserved my wish to be able to continue school up to A level and to study medicine afterwards. It is quite normal for young people to have big dreams about their future career, but they at that stage cannot judge whether they would be suitable for it. So I cannot tell at all, even now, whether I would really have been qualified for that esteemed profession. But at least in the course of time I had experiences, completely unplanned, which showed me that I was not completely untalented, at least on the practical side. Three times altogether I took over the task of a midwife during births, although I had no training for it. The first case happened in 2009, when I was nearby when a cousin went into labour and she called me for help. This was also the most serious case I experienced, because it was a breech birth[7]. Despite the considerable difficulties involved, I managed to bring the child into the world alive. In 2013, a Southern Sudanese refugee woman called me when her contractions began. She trusted me very much. It turned out that she was pregnant with twins, but the birth itself was not a big problem. However, there was not even a thread available to bind the umbilical cord. Without further ado, I tore off some strong stalks in the grass in front of the hut, with which I achieved the same purpose. A third case occurred in 2014, when a neighbour was in labour. Here, too, I was called in because no midwife was available and the woman trusted me. Everything went well. Despite the unusual demands, it was always a matter of course for me to take on the tasks I was given. I was not afraid, rather it

---

[7] A breech birth is when the baby is not born head first, but with legs and buttocks in front. This can lead to complications, by obstructing the oxygen supply to the baby's brain. If no medical support is available, the baby or even both mother and child may die.

satisfied me to tackle the problems and to be able to cope with them.

But I never got the chance to pursue my real professional goal. The necessary money was not available and the necessities of everyday life were always so pressing that I could not take any serious steps in that direction anyway. So this ambition gradually receded more and more into the background.

However, I was always willing to try and learn something new, and also to adapt to difficult situations. So I never gave up but always trusted that, with God's help, I could achieve something in the end. For half a year I had no other choice but to concentrate again on supporting my family. I got together with a good friend and we started a joint trade baking really delicious cakes. We complemented each other very well. With these cakes we went from market to market every day and earned quite a bit of money. However, after some time my girlfriend had to give up the business because she got sick and I could not find anyone else who was equally suitable for this business. It was not possible for me to run this trade alone. So I had to find something else for my living.

Why and How I Came to South Sudan

For a while I worked in a hair salon as a hairdresser. But it was clear from the beginning that this would not be for long. One of my customers there became my good friend. She worked as a supervisor in the Gulu office of the American development aid organization USAID. One day – it was in mid 2015 – she told me that USAID was looking for teachers for a school project in South Sudan, where there was civil war, and she asked if this was perhaps something for me.

The USAID BRAC project was intended to help young people in South Sudan to receive an education, albeit an extremely basic one. South Sudan had become independent in 2011, after years of unrest. In 2013, the civil war began in full force, but even before that, there had always been armed conflicts, which particularly affected the civilian population. As a result, only half of school-age children actually attended school. The civil war then led to an enormous increase in the number of refugees, to the closure of more than 1,000 schools throughout the country and to a situation where a large proportion of children grew up in camps that provided hardly any specific support for them. The USAID project aimed to give a total of 10,500 pupils – refugees and non-refugees – in selected districts of South Sudan the opportunity to receive an education. There was a focus on girls, because they were at an additional disadvantage compared to boys. A total of 350 community schools were to be established. The idea of a "community school" is that it should be not only a place of education, but also serves as a social services centre for the surrounding area.

Suitable personnel were sought for the implementation of this project. I applied and, due to the recommendation by my friend and after an interview, I was chosen to work in this project, in the field of education, not in that of social work. Although formally I was only qualified for a job as a teacher in a kindergarten, my contract from the beginning provided that I would work there as a primary school teacher. I was offered an initial salary of $100 a month, which was quite attractive at the time. That amount is still more than what an elementary school teacher with formal training now receives as starting salary in Gulu. I was overjoyed, because the job appealed to me very much. On the one hand, I urgently needed a permanent paid job for my own livelihood and the support of my family; on the other hand, I wanted to get out of my very restrictive environment in Gulu, where I could not develop further. It was particularly appealing for me to have the opportunity to work with disadvantaged children.

Life and Work in South Sudan

My contract said that I would work in connection with refugee camps for a period of three years and with the possibility of an extension. I underwent some courses, in teaching and classroom management as well as in the subjects I was expected to teach. Originally, it had been anticipated that I would go to the South Sudanese capital, Juba, but the security situation there had become so catastrophic that the plan was dropped. So instead I was sent to Nimule. This place is not far from the border with Uganda – Gulu could be reached by bus in little more than one hour – and one of the reasons why it had been chosen was that, in the event of a crisis, protection could be sought quickly on the other side of the border. During my mission in Nimule, we often heard gunfire from the surrounding area, but thank God the fighting did not reach the town. Nevertheless, life there was dangerous. For example we were urged never to go into the rural surroundings of Nimule, because mines had been laid everywhere.

In Nimule itself the population had a critical attitude towards life. By this I mean that people were much more aggressive than I was used to from my own ethnic group, which in itself is already far from being always peaceful. But the majority of the local men living in Nimule had no other occupation than being soldiers or serving in civil war militias. They all possessed firearms and they were quick-tempered. If they were angry with anyone, they could easily go home, get their guns and shoot the person they were angry with. So you had to be very vigilant all the time to feel when a situation became critical, and we were told it was best to withdraw quickly if you were not very sure of being able to solve the problem yourself, and safely.

When I was sent to this place, strangely enough it had been assumed that the local population there belonged to the South Sudanese branch of my own tribe, the Acholi or Luo, so I would not have to expect language problems in daily practice. That was wrong information, maybe due to the fact that the shift of the place of operation from Juba to Nimule came at short notice. So it was only when I stood in front of the class for the first time that it turned out that we did not understand each other at all! The local population, from which some of my students came, belonged mostly to the Madi tribe, whose language was totally different from mine. The majority of the students were refugees who spoke a selection of very different languages as used in South Sudan, for example Dinka.

The only language they all had in common was a

basic knowledge of Sudanese Arabic. While most South Sudanese are Catholic or Anglican Christians, in Nimule itself, in the shops and in many key positions, there were Muslims who originally came from the Sudanese capital Khartoum and they spoke only Arabic. Both for communication with my students and for everyday life, I therefore had to learn this language as quickly as possible, even if only to a highly imperfect degree.

One of the given goals for our classes was that the students should learn English and a few of them already had a little bit of previous knowledge. With the others I had to start from scratch. As soon as a sufficient level of knowledge was reached, I taught in English whenever possible. It was also in this language that the pupils learned how to write and read. Those who know me will be aware that my own English is also full of flaws (I had help to write down this story). But the aim here was not to qualify the elite for university, but to give very poor, uprooted children – most of them girls – at least some initial knowledge that could be helpful in their future lives.

Using the regular educational material for Ugandan schools (we never had enough) I had to teach all subjects: mathematics, English, science, and social studies. The teaching conditions were very basic. A total of twelve project schools had been set up in the Nimule area and just one teacher had been hired for each of them. My school was merely a makeshift residential building that had been rented for these purposes. We had a blackboard, but neither chairs nor tables; we sat on mats on the floor. There was only one class with 30 students, aged seven to twelve or thirteen years, and they all had the same lessons together. My mission was to elevate these pupils from one level of primary school to the next within eight months each, i.e. continuously from Primary 1 to Primary 2 and up to Primary 3. At regular schools, with much better conditions, one year is standard for each of these steps. I had been told as an explanation that the project objective was, as far as my particular task was concerned, to enable the children to complete Primary 3. But the available funds, as well as the approved time period for implementing the task, were not sufficient to carry out the teaching that was necessary for this. I have no idea who made the mistake, why and when, but we were actually burdened with an almost impossible task. Nevertheless, I somehow managed to meet the targets set for me. The children took a test at the end of each class, which was limited to the content that we had actually been able to go through. The children had put so much effort into it and deserved formal recognition for their efforts, even though it was clear to me and the teachers at the other schools that this qualification was not comparable to that of a formal school under orderly conditions.

It was already difficult enough for me to look after this one school effectively. But then it happened that two of my colleagues at nearby schools dropped out due to pregnancy and I also had to take over their classes for several months. This meant an enormous extra burden on my time and left me hardly any time alone. I taught every day from early morning to early evening, two classes in the morning and one in the afternoon. To prepare myself properly for the classes of the following day was hardly possible. I often just had to go ahead together with the students, following the sequence of the teaching material, and was forced to understand quickly from the books what I was expected to teach. Furthermore, these other schools were for slightly older children up to Primary 7, i.e. with completely different content to the lessons. As if that wasn't enough, I also became supervisor of the other colleagues in the area, which meant taking over some additional administrative tasks, too.

I adapted to these unexpected demands as best I could and received recognition from the students as well as the parents (where there were any – this was by no means a matter of course in view of the fate of the refugees). However, under the enormous mental stress I almost collapsed and even in bed at night I could not get away from thinking of the kids and the lessons.

One of the more memorable events of that time was when a fourteen-year-old boy student seriously asked me to marry him. His proposal wasn't the only one I received in Nimule – more about that later – but this was the only one which had something touching about it.

Back to my own actual class: Since the project had a focus on the promotion of female students, the majority of my students were girls. We were popular with their parents, because our school did not charge school fees, which in many cases the parents would have been reluctant to spend on girls. However, as co-education was also part of the concept, it would have been unacceptable if I had chosen the easy way by running the school with girls alone. So I did a lot of persuading, for example at the parent meetings, to send me the boys of the families as well. In the end I was successful and one third of my students were male.

Because of the great heterogeneity of the group, it was very important to arrange the seating arrangement so that no disturbances occurred. I made the children sit on the floor in a U-shape and I sat or stood in the opening of this U, so that I always had everyone in view. The seating arrangement was two girls one boy, two girls one boy, etc. As soon as I got to know the pupils a little better, I put them together in a thought-through way so that no cliques were formed and so that frictions were minimized. But the latter could not be avoided completely and once, when I turned my back to the class to write on the blackboard, one girl attacked another and scratched her face. Both children reported this to their parents, who then positioned themselves against each other and also became aggressive towards me. This was awkward, but a respected local man, who was called in by the project management, mediated very well. The parents apologized to me and the father of the girl who had started the aggression paid compensation to the family of the other girl. This was a happy ending, because even such seemingly insignificant situations could have easily escalated.

But other situations I experienced were even more delicate and they were partly connected with the fact that I, as a single, young and – as it seemed – appealing woman, excited the imagination of some men too much. For example, there was a tall and very strong police officer in Nimule who wanted me to marry his son, who was training in Australia at the time but, according to his father, had the possibility of a great career later. The father offered to take me into his family immediately, and the formal marriage could take place after his son's return. I turned him down flat on the grounds that no one could know whether we would find each other attractive if we were to meet one day. The father seemed to accept it and for me the matter was settled.

But when I was still in bed late in the morning one free weekend, this police officer in full uniform and armed with his gun came to the one-room hut where I lived with a colleague of mine. He gave her some money so she would go to the village and buy drinks. No sooner had she left the hut than he sat down on my bed, began to paw me and said that he loved me. I told him to leave me alone immediately or I would scream loudly and then he would get into trouble in his position. "Oh," he said, "you are so beautiful, many more men will die because of you." I replied that I did not want to hear such nonsense and that he should keep his hands off me. Instead he took out his pistol and waved it threateningly in my face. Thank God my colleague came back at that very moment. Together we angrily called him names and forced him out. I complained about him to the local authorities and he was transferred to another place.

It was commonplace to be harassed by men on the street – sometimes just getting overdone compliments, requests for dates or straightforward proposals for marriage – but very often also being insulted in a very vulgar way. Especially if you were recognized as a woman from Uganda, you were often told that all Ugandan women were prostitutes and only spread HIV. Ugandan women were regarded as fair game. And it did not stop at harassment in public, where there were normally at least some other people watching and perhaps preventing the situation from becoming really dangerous. One day a young man broke into my hut, declared that he wanted to marry me and immediately started harassing me physically. I rejected him, whereupon he loudly cursed me in the worst possible way and continued to harass me physically, now in an even harsher way. Although I am slim, I have always been a good sportswoman and am stronger than people expect me to be. In addition, as mentioned, I went through a hard school in the refugee camp during my childhood where I had to assert myself again and again, also physically. I had not forgotten these experiences and still knew how to assess critical situations in order to be able to behave appropriately.

In this case, the necessary reaction was clear and I acted so quickly that it brought me the advantage of surprise: I simply grabbed the man, dragged him to the entrance and pushed him out with verve. He was sitting stunned outside in the dust of the street yelling, "No woman can do this to me! I'll punish you!" But a local man confronted him and said he heard exactly what happened. The treatment I gave him was, so he explained, the only right thing to do and the guy should not dare to hurt me under any circumstances. And so it actually happened. But more than that, the rejected lover later on saw himself as my friend and protector. Sometimes he would warn other men not to approach me: "Be careful, this woman is very dangerous!"

A cousin of mine had married a man from South

Sudan and ran a small snack bar in Nimule. When I had time on weekends, I sometimes helped her a bit. Once when I was in the kitchen, I heard my cousin's excited voice from the main room and went to her. She was arguing with a guest who had drunk several bottles of beer and now wanted to leave without paying. I said to him, "You pay now or you'll get in trouble." He just said laughingly, "What are you, as a woman, going to do?" and set about leaving the restaurant. Thereupon I pushed him to the ground and fought with him so violently that he got quite a few scratches and scrapes. Finally, he was lying on his back, I kneeled upon him and tore the shoes off his feet. "You'll only get them back if you pay," I told him. He cursed terribly in Arabic and I gave him back accordingly in the same language. But in the end, he actually paid. He continued from time to time to come to this restaurant for a drink, but from now on he always paid in advance and when he saw me he showed great respect. These were unpleasant experiences, but nothing happened to me. They could have ended quite differently.

I had a very close relationship with my students, loved them almost as if they were my own children and received a lot of affection from them. This contributed greatly to the fact that the children were very happy to go to school, because they felt comfortable with me – unfortunately often in contrast to what they experienced at home. It was very nice to see how hard they tried to learn and how they wanted to show that to me. It made me happy to see their progress and that spurred them on even more.

Every morning before classes started, we sat

together and I asked the children what was new and what they had experienced. Several of these children were orphans because their parents had been killed in the civil war. I also heard stories related to that. I especially remember the story of one girl: she had lived in the capital, Juba, and one day, as so often, gunshots could be heard. But this time it was particularly violent and finally it became clear that members of a militia were going from house to house and shooting the inhabitants. The girl's parents said that they had to leave quickly before these guys came to their house. But then, when the family was outside, they were immediately shot at and the parents were killed. The girl managed to escape in the direction of the river, the Nile, where she wanted to hide in the shallow water at a place protected by overhanging trees. But there the whole bank was full of corpses and blood. Countless murdered people of all ages and sexes lay on top of and below each other, often dismembered. It was simply horrible. The girl told me that ever since she saw those mountains of human flesh, she could never eat meat again.

My contract for the assignment in Nimule didn't provide for a vacation. I only had free time on weekends but since the drive from there to Gulu took more than one hour and as I needed some peaceful time for myself, I didn't go home very often.

In that time, an important change had happened: a family in Gulu – they were of Dinka, i.e. South Sudanese origin – had contacted my mother. They said that they could imagine that I would be a good wife for their son, because according to them I was not only good-looking but also had a good personality. My mother passed this on to me. I thought the young man in question was actually quite nice and we had known each other since our school days. I could imagine falling in love with him. It was also a good family, although poor like us. Anyway, I was tired of having men chasing me all the time and I thought that at 23 years of age I was old enough to start my own family, which would give me a stable support for whatever would come in future. So I gave my consent and we had a traditional marriage in early 2016, with the appropriate rituals.

Such a traditional marriage differs from a marriage at the registry office in that, although being legal, it is not registered according to civil law and only provides customary rights and duties. Adding civil marriage as a second step is something that most people in my tribe, and probably elsewhere in Uganda, do without. One reason for this is that it is common in our culture for a man to have several wives. This is also expressly permitted by law. However, once he is formally married according to civil law and a church wedding has also taken place, it is not acceptable to take any more wives. Such formal marriages, if they exist at all, therefore, often take place between the man and his first wife only after the two have been married the traditional way for a long time and their children are also grown up, because then the man would normally not want to take any more wives. I know from conversations that this is very difficult for people from the West to understand, but they should not be outraged by it. First of all, they should know that we have a large surplus of female births to male births, which is precisely why there are many more women than men of marriageable age. So when a man takes several wives, he is helping to make family life possible for women who otherwise would not have a chance to do so.

Rather a short time after the marriage, I went back to Nimule and my husband went back to South Sudan, where his family came from, and he worked as a craftsman in a place very far away from Nimule. So we hardly lived together at all in the months after our marriage. But I soon realized that I had already become pregnant in the short time we were together. I continued my work nevertheless and would have been very happy to return to Nimule after maternity leave, which according to my contract would have encompassed two months before and one month after birth. I would have left the care of my child to my mother-in-law. Arrangements like this are common in Uganda.

But while we were working to help the youth of South Sudan to achieve a better future for themselves and others, the news about the terrible things that were happening there during the civil war became more and more frequent and the armed conflicts moved closer and closer to our area of operations. It was therefore decided by the aid agency to cancel the teachers' contracts and to end the project there, because the risk simply could not be borne any more – and so I returned to Gulu. It broke my heart having to let my students stay there alone. I had become very important for them and they had enriched my own life so much. I don't know what happened to any of them afterwards. Now I stayed with my husband's family for a year, took care of my beloved child and helped my mother-in-law. My husband from time to time came to visit us.

Working in a Refugee Camp in Uganda

It depressed me, however, that I could no longer financially support my family of origin, who were really in need. In addition, I was not satisfied in the long run with being at home all the time doing nothing but household chores. Therefore I became excited when, after being back for one year, I saw another advertisement by the NGO Save the Children for interesting positions, including social worker and teacher positions for people with O level qualifications. I reacted immediately. The work was various childcare positions – both teaching and social care – in one of the refugee camps in Adjumani, a town at the White Nile, on the border with South Sudan.

Uganda is home to the largest number of refugees in Africa – 1.4 million people, many of them from South Sudan. These people are often unable to return home for years or they even stay for good as they don't have other alternatives. Uganda tries to integrate them into its own society, for example by making land available to them. In order to support this integration process, efforts have been made to provide them with preparatory support during their stay in refugee camps. This also included teaching the children. The needed finance came from government and foreign aid. I don't know who provided most.

I applied and underwent a lengthy interview. My experience with refugee life, my knowledge of various languages and my positive attitude towards children impressed the interviewers. So I was hired as teacher for the nursery, with direct responsibility for pre-school, i.e. for the children aged 5-6 years. My salary was 300,000 Ugandan Shillings (equivalent to about 78 US$) a month, which is on the same level as what regular Ugandan teachers at primary schools receive in the beginning. From this salary I also had to pay the rent for a hut to live in and for my food. During the time I worked in Adjumani my daughter was looked after by my mother-in-law and her family. I must say they loved me and my child. My husband continued working in South Sudan and we did not meet very often, but in my mind it was clear that we nevertheless belonged together and that I loved him.

The local population in Adjumani were mostly Ugandan Madi. Some of their kids were also attending my school. The composition of the refugee camp population, which contributed the majority of the pupils, was even more heterogeneous than the population in Nimule. Unlike in Nimule, there were also internal refugees from Uganda with different ethnic and therefore also linguistic backgrounds. This surprised me somewhat, as the civil war in Uganda had largely subsided after a peace accord in 2006, but now, in 2017, reintegration at national level was apparently still not complete. The majority of the refugees at that camp, and thus also of my students, came from South Sudan. Among them were many Sudanese Madi and it turned out to be a great advantage that in Nimule I had already learned their language to some extent, as well as that of their Dinka rivals who were also strongly represented in the camp. But there were also members of other Sudanese tribes, including Sudanese Luo, i.e. from the Acholi ethnic group from whose Ugandan branch I came. Each of these tribes has its own language. But in Adjumani, like before, in Nimule, we used English as the general language as far as possible.

In the first year the lessons took place in a big tent, but unlike in Nimule, we had chairs and tables. In the second year the Japanese government provided the financial means for us to rent two classrooms and an office in one building, which made teaching much easier. The work with the children went largely without problems, but it was the parents who sometimes caused us difficulties. For example, it was not uncommon that when another child was born into a family, they would take their kindergarten child out of school, no matter whether it was a girl or a boy, to take care of the newborn.

There was also a problem of mentality, which was explained by the fact that most of those refugees who had been living in refugee camps for years, had become accustomed to being cared for, and they claimed benefits to which they believed they were entitled. Thus, it was by no means an isolated incident that parent meetings were not attended or that the parents immediately left unless drinks and snacks were provided for them. They were used to this service through various rather wealthy aid organizations. However, times had changed, many NGOs had ceased working in Uganda and most which stayed were forced to practice austerity. So we teachers, too, had not been provided with funds for entertaining participants at meetings and it was unthinkable that we teachers and social workers should pay from our meagre salaries for hospitality for the parents. But the parents had no understanding for that.

We generally did not have the feeling that – in view of our difficult living and working conditions – the people in charge of the project had thought enough about how they could have supported us in everyday matters. For example, although we had a heavy workload already, we always had to walk, in the heat, four or five kilometres to another place to collect our salary.

Life in the refugee camp was unfortunately disturbed by ethnic tensions. The predominant host community outside of the borders of the camp, i.e. local Ugandan Madi, did not like the members of other tribes very much, while the Madi refugees from South Sudan within our camp felt strengthened through this relation. My impression was that the Madi are not very friendly anyway. Maybe I had some prejudices because of what I knew about our history in which there had been armed fights between the Madi and my tribe, the Acholi, but although I very consciously wanted to open up to them, I unfortunately found my prejudice somewhat confirmed in practice.

The Dinka, in particular, suffered from discrimination. In large areas of South Sudan, the Dinka are predominant and the Madi are in the minority. Here it was the other way round. The Dinka were aware that they were guests in a foreign country and that they were surrounded by a different ethnic group that was not necessarily friendly to them. They therefore made a special effort to be reserved and were willing to subordinate themselves. Nevertheless, when their women went out into the open country outside the camp to collect firewood or cut grass, they were often insulted by the locals: this is our land and you have no business here. It was not unusual for women to report that they had been raped.

But the Dinka also had their own peculiarities that made my work difficult. The parents made it clear to me that their culture did not allow boys to sit next to girls even at kindergarten age and they insisted on strict separation. And again the ethnic segregation: the children of different origins always wanted to sit together with children from the same tribe and have nothing to do with the others. I did not get involved in this but said that we are all brothers and sisters and together we have experienced the fate of expulsion. Then they might accept having to sit together in class, but without any social contact, and when I left the room after class, they separated again immediately. That was very disappointing for me.

But the segregation according to ethnic origin was not only evident among the refugees and the simple local population, but even among the Ugandan teachers. These came from a wide variety of ethnic groups, too. It is said that there are 40 or more different tribes or ethnic groups in Uganda, speaking a great variety of often very different languages, each of these groups with its own history that is often full of stories about violent fights with other tribes. The loyalty of the citizens in Uganda, at least outside the capital Kampala, belongs first and foremost to their own clan and tribe and only secondarily, with quite some distance, to the country.

After some time, I became the lead teacher, assigned to this position through a vote among the teachers and also with the consent of the supervisor from the NGO.

This also meant that I had a certain disciplinary authority. There were teachers who did not take their job seriously and sometimes did not show up for duty, maybe for a whole week. But they still expected me to mark their presence on the worksheet for that time. I refused and they did not receive a salary for the period when they had not worked. The accusations I received in response to this were very often based on my ethnicity, on the basis of which I allegedly discriminated against others, supported by our higher supervisor who shared the same ethnicity with me. In fact, it was jealousy and a lack of work motivation that led to these conflicts. Thankfully, I really was very much supported in my position by the supervisor from the NGO, but it was not because of the shared ethnic background but only because we both were trying to achieve good results. I was very concerned about how much this tribal thinking affected professional work. I recently heard that even today in colleges in the USA it is often the case that at mealtimes black and white students prefer to sit down with others of the same skin colour rather than just sit down somewhere where there is room. If this is true, I find it very sad and I wonder how integration can really succeed if this kind of separation can remain in effect even after such a long common history.

In Adjumani, too, as in Nimule, I had very good contact with the children. We enjoyed being together very much. They often came from very difficult backgrounds, on the one hand because of the events of the civil war and the flight – although these young children often had not experienced this directly, being born in the camp – but on the other hand also because of the family circumstances. There were groups among the refugees where the parents did not care much for their children and this was then evident in the children. I remember a five-year-old girl who was very timid. I tried very hard to gain her trust and when I succeeded, she was obviously overjoyed to have found someone to whom she could speak openly. It turned out that she was regularly physically abused at home. She had a fairly large wound on her back from being beaten. We had very strict child protection rules and so I went with the child to her parents and made it clear that they were now under observation and that they would face serious sanctions if further maltreatment occurred. They obviously were intimidated by this. We monitored the effect of this admonition on a regular and long-term basis and did not find signs of mistreatment any more. The girl gradually revived more and more.

My private life in Adjumani was unobtrusive in that I was very much focused on my work there. Like in Nimule, I lived in a traditional simple thatched African hut. Everything could have been peaceful if I had not been subjected to multiple harassments again. My expectation that as a married woman I would be met with greater restraint was hardly fulfilled. On the contrary, many seemed to assume that I urgently needed a replacement for my absent husband. Men from the Dinka tribe even told me that it was a good tradition among them to take "loving" care of a woman who was temporarily without her husband. This, they said, brings with it a form of protection from the man who occupies that position. I explained that there is no such tradition in my tribe and I did not want to adapt to it. I said I was also able to defend myself. That is what I did. Unlike in Nimule, unambiguous forceful words were enough for this – physical confrontations were not necessary.

I worked in that camp for refugees from South Sudan for nearly two years and would have liked to continue doing so. However, my husband was very much caught up in traditional ideas. Although he was absent abroad himself most of the time, he did not like the fact that I was working independently and far away from his family's home. He therefore contacted the project management and demanded that the contract with me be terminated. I had no other choice than to return to Gulu. I wanted to do my best to make him happy and to safeguard our love.

Not long after my return, my husband came home one day accompanied by two young, pregnant women, totally unknown to me and very unfriendly in their attitude. He told me that these were his two new wives, but I would of course remain in the leading position as wife number one. As mentioned before, it is customary in Uganda for many men to have more than one wife. I also knew that my husband had had two brothers who had died as children. In his tribe, in such a case, it is even considered a kind of obligation to take additional wives, who are then symbolically considered wives of the deceased brothers, and the children are then also attributed to them.

So I knew that this issue would probably come up one day. And, in principle, I thought that I would not reject this right from the beginning, as long as certain rules were kept. These rules, in a good family, include that the man is able to maintain such an extended family in the first place and that such a decision is made together. When the man has such thoughts, he talks to his first wife and she tells him what kind of women she thinks would fit into the family and which would not. Sometimes they also choose these women together, or at least she has a right to object. Always completely indisputable should be the fact that the first wife remains the most important person on the female side and that with her all threads converge. The new wives do not live together with the original couple under one roof, but are each given their own hut and the husband decides, after consultation with his first wife, when he will stay in each of the other huts. Strict adherence to the rules is a prerequisite to avoid jealousy. All these rules, however, had been disregarded in this case and my husband confronted me with these already-pregnant women, who I found personally unpleasant. It was degrading and I realized abruptly that I could not possibly come to terms with this situation.

I told my husband at that time that his behaviour was a great breach of faith, due to which I had irretrievably lost trust in him. Looking back now, with some distance of time from the incident, I believe that at least equally significant was the fact that – even though I had expected this situation – when it came to it, my whole feeling revolted against such a scenario – venerable traditions or not. I was simply unable to come to terms emotionally with the fact that, from now on, I would always share my husband with other women that I would see every day. This was a very personal decision, not one I made out of theoretical considerations about female emancipation in Africa. My love for my husband had died because of his attitude, and so I left him. He as well as his family did not want to allow it at all, but I prevailed. The dowry that my mother had received for me – most of the agreed amount had remained unpaid anyhow – was returned. After a few months, but only when I threatened to get the police involved, I finally managed to get my daughter to stay with me. My ex-husband has since tried several times to persuade me to return, but I have no feelings for him anymore. He now has five children from different women.

My Life Today

The civil war in Uganda has largely abated, and international mediation has also led to a certain calming of the political and military situation in Southern Sudan. From NGO circles I heard that this also has the consequence that now not so much foreign money is flowing any more to support the refugees and to promote our economic development. This, they say, is due to dwindling interest from abroad. But even where international organizations would still be prepared to make funds available, in many or even most cases they insist the Ugandan Government make a counterpart contribution to the financing of projects. However, the government is allegedly claiming budget difficulties, especially now under coronavirus conditions, and that is why some projects do not come about.

These financial constraints are added to the fact that poverty is still widespread, particularly in the north and thus also in the Gulu region, that there are far too few jobs and that the integration of refugees, including internally displaced persons, is far from complete. South Sudan is the poorest country in the world and offers its population even fewer prospects than we have in Gulu, so there is little incentive for refugees in Uganda to return to South Sudan. In any case, the demand for staff with my qualifications has fallen, as activities of the kind I previously was involved in have declined due to the lack of funds for relevant projects.

Again I live in a traditional thatched round hut. It is located on the outskirts of the city of Gulu. The area does not have a very good reputation, but I cannot afford a better environment. I would not be able to live on the salary of a nursery teacher. I now have to take care of my daughter alone – as happened with my mother when her husband left, my ex-husband does not pay anything for our mutual child – and I also support relatives, in particular my mother and my younger half-brother, who is still at school. Therefore, before the coronavirus crisis started in 2020, I had started small-scale business work again, for example buying used clothes in bulk from Europe in the Ugandan capital, Kampala, and selling them at the market in Gulu. That is a difficult and also risky business. In Kampala I was attacked and beaten up by a group of youngsters who then ran away with my bag and the money. This was a very serious setback for me. In another case I helped arrange a church fete in Gulu and asked friends to watch my bag for a limited time. But when I returned, the friends were gone and the wallet in my bag was empty. I have become very careful now of trusting people.

However, recently I was very lucky to be able to borrow a little money to set up a very simple and very small grocery shop in a poor part of the town. I entered this new task with a lot of energy and confidence. However, it turned out that I can add very little to the price at which I buy the goods myself from the wholesaler. There is also a lot of competition. This makes it very difficult to earn a sufficient profit. Although my store is open seven days a week and I work from dawn to dusk, sometimes assisted by one of my brothers or my brother-in-law, I just manage to cover the costs of the store but barely have enough surplus to pay the rent for my hut as well. I continue to look for ways to increase the attractiveness of my business so that more people will buy from me. As an alternative, together with friends, I am thinking of buying agricultural products in the villages and acting as a wholesaler myself. But we don't have the necessary capital.

Before coronavirus changed everything, part of my routine was attending church every Sunday. Sometimes I also ran the Sunday school and from time to time I was even asked to speak to the parish and lead the prayers. I hope that I can pick up where I left off there soon.

Towards the end of 2019 I became a volunteer worker for the local NGO GWAD (Grassroots Women's and Men's Association for Development). It was founded in 1998 to work with women and children in the refugee camps. Today, it is particularly committed to improving the living conditions of the very poor rural women in the Gulu area. Most of them were formerly residents of camps for internal refugees. Recently, the NGO's activities have been extended to men, because we believe in cooperation between men and women and in the need for mutual support. This is also where I can contribute my varied experience, and I have noticed that I can easily communicate with the rural population because I understand them and their situation very well. I also learn a lot myself. This activity is very satisfying, although we are extremely short of money, because we have no foreign sponsors, and, furthermore, due to the coronavirus pandemic we are currently largely unable to undertake activities. I have to admit, though, that I had to cut back on these activities a lot anyhow after I opened my own small business.

A girlfriend who read the draft of my story suggested that I add the following episode because she thinks it is characteristic of me. There is a radio show in Uganda regularly discussing relationship problems. Some months ago I sent the presenter a comment on a discussion. He then did a telephone interview with me, which was also broadcast. It had to do with how to deal with certain critical situations in a relationship. I was particularly sensitized at the time because my marriage had just failed. On the basis of this interview I received a whole series of reactions from listeners who felt positively addressed. Some asked me for advice for their own lives. My girlfriend says that I have a certain talent for dealing with people, especially for inspiring their trust, and according to her it was a pity that I could not make a more intensive use of this talent. Perhaps there is some truth to that. I like working with people and I enjoy when something I do for myself helps others at the same time.

Epilogue

The security situation in Gulu and other parts of Northern Uganda has improved greatly since the civil war subsided. However, it remains a region with a lot of people living in extreme poverty, with a population growth rate that exceeds economic growth and with far too few jobs. Women are disadvantaged in many ways. The crime rate is high and being on the streets during darkness is very risky, not only for women.

Serious infectious diseases are rampant in our country. Thus, diseases have led to my mother losing three of her children in the course of time. When my father died in 2008, three of the five additional children he had fathered after separating from my mother had already died. I had malaria several times, and in 2019 I almost died of typhoid fever. In 2020 my three-year-old daughter contracted malaria tropica and had already fallen into a coma when she was rescued at the last minute by a quinine injection, which was medically risky because of her young age.

This story, despite difficult overall conditions, is one of distinctly personal experiences, and I have restricted myself very largely to what I remember and what I know myself. A friend has added a few notes to give helpful background information to selected points but I didn't want too much to be added that only comes from books.

It came as a surprise when an acquaintance, who I had told a little about my previous life, asked me to write down my experiences so that they could be published. I gladly admit that I am pleased about this. I have experienced a lot and have dealt with it in my own personal way in order to exist. The questions I was asked and the ones I am now asking myself have led me to remember and reassess the details of my life described here. I am grateful for the opportunity that I was given to share my experiences with others and I wonder what they might think about them.

Yes, I have gone through some quite bitter experiences, but I don't know phases of lasting mental depression. Instead I mostly was a joyous, sociable person and, before the recent lockdown, was open for simple entertainment like dancing etc. I also see my story as an example of the many fates, full of stress, danger, shortcomings and failures that have happened to so many people in this region. And it is not over at all. Events like those I have described are still happening today.

Visualizing Change: The road to ensuring that no one on earth will die from preventable diseases

José Zea and Laura Velásquez (Colombia)

"Laurita!" he screamed enthusiastically. "Thank you for loving my grandson." And he would give me a warm hug. That's how he was with me every time I saw him. That's what I remember most about him. In 2018 the doctor said everything would have been different if we had noticed it earlier. Unfortunately, there was nothing to be done any more. "His cancer is so advanced, and soon he will die." That was the last thing the doctor said to José, my co-founder, leaving him surprised, sad, and helpless to know that his grandfather had cancer and that there was nothing to be done. He had belatedly been diagnosed with a tumor in his liver that none of his doctors had noticed for months.

In my case, things weren't different. Soon I was going through the same scenario. However, instead of receiving just one late diagnosis in my family, I experienced the death of three of my grandparents. In less than three months, I had lost the three pillars of my life, and for the same reason José's grandfather had just passed away: with a late diagnosis.

José was very worried, and in many conversations he asked me why his grandfather's cancer had not been detected in time; why, if we have specialists, if we pay for a good health service, it was not noticed. "What could we do to help him?" he asked. "I have an idea," he told me. "I have been looking for ways to help my grandfather lead a better lifestyle in this little time he has left. Do you want to help me? Look what I found." He sent me several links with information on health and behavioural changes to prevent diseases. I was surprised. We found a lot of scary statistics, which made us curious, so we continued studying. I realized that what was happening to his grandfather was precisely the same thing that was happening to my grandparents, a late diagnosis that was ending my grandparents' lives.

In the midst of all this, José told me, "I have been

researching, and there are ways to prevent diseases by changing behaviours that can help us lead a better lifestyle. What do you think if we try to do something for ourselves? My dad (Elias, who is a doctor) can help us in the process." Without thinking about it, we started a very long research process, so many trials and so many errors to see what might work to somehow help what was going on. However, in a matter of time, José's grandfather died, too soon to try what we were building.

After these events and after much research, we had understood that the biggest challenge in the global health industry is prevention and early diagnosis. So, tired of waiting to do something, José, his father and I created a chatbot to help people detect and prevent chronic diseases such as diabetes and cardiovascular diseases. It was a free AI coach that you would find on Facebook Messenger. In less than a month, we had more than 9,000 users in 22 countries. The chatbot was a risk classifier of these pathologies, using data from people's behaviours. Basically, we collected data from your smart phone and asked you about your daily life, how you ate, your stress level, if you were physically active and how you slept.

We often sat down to write to each of these users, and we found many sad insights. Among many, we found a lack of education around health; for example, many asked us if diabetes was contagious. On one occasion, a young woman asked us if we could help her father, who was diabetic and an alcoholic. She told us that her father had suffered an accident and had no access to a hospital because she lived in a remote village. Her father had fallen, and his head was bleeding. She did not know what to do or how to help him; she asked us desperately what to do. We didn't know how to help her at the time. After a few days, she wrote to us that her father had died and that she could not help him because he didn't have access to a hospital. However, the most unfortunate thing we found is that there is a massive gap in access to the healthcare system in the world. From there, we understood that, beyond just helping others, there was a huge opportunity and the problem was much bigger than we had imagined.

Despite not knowing anything about healthcare, despite not knowing how to write a single line of code, we decided to start and create a technology company dedicated to the healthcare industry. José finished his master's degree and worked full time for our company, Arkangel AI. Elias was the medical lead at all times, and I quit my job, and started working full time too. We decided to work in Canada, hoping to understand how artificial intelligence could help us solve the big problems we had encountered with these 9,000 users, and what better place than where this AI technology was born?

From then, the story was different. We embarked on a mission to create a start-up that would help people live free of preventable diseases – without knowing where to start or having the proper knowledge to do so. However, the purpose was so real that we had no doubts. We went through the most challenging times as entrepreneurs. Like every entrepreneur, we worked 24/7. We applied to endless accelerators, incubators, innovation programmes, and all industries, hoping for guidance. After many efforts, we got into two accelerators, which gave us the tools to build a path with the foundations we had already walked. While we were not experts in the industry, we did have knowledge in other areas that helped us move forward. From this moment on, we also had a structure. We had a minimum viable product, which validated the market problem. However, we were missing a lot of aspects to be able to reach our objective. We needed clinical studies and pilot tests to comply with many regulations, and we required a lot of money to do this.

As a result, we decided that the best option was to contact people in the industry who could validate the usability of what we were developing. That's how we went to one of the great accelerator programmes at the best university in Canada. That gave us tools in start-up creation, business modelling and scientific validation – everything that comes with creating a company – and we were selected to go to the most important innovation centres in the world to present Arkangel AI. We went to Silicon Valley, Boston, New York, London and many other places.

During this tour, we became experts in making pitches, connecting with people, and finding answers to our questions. However, it was one of the most difficult challenges. We received many "no"s, many answers like "what you do has no value," or "you cannot do what you do if you do not have knowledge on the subject," and we also received many comments like "in a market like this if you are Latino and there is a woman as co-founder you do not have many opportunities." It was a challenge – medically, scientifically, as entrepreneurs and as people. However, we didn't stop, but we did understand that many of these insights, tips, and conversations that we gathered translated into something precious for us. It had clarified for us that if you don't have control over what happens outside the patient's clinical environment, there are many risks, which made it very complex to fulfil our purpose.

When we were on our way back, we felt that what we were doing had no head or tail. And yet, there was a snowball growing with thousands of people writing to us every day looking for answers. As a team, we saw a very dark reality. We were going blindly down a path and we didn't yet know where to go. But at least we were together to keep figuring out that path.

With all that we had learned, we understood that the biggest challenge for the healthcare industry is to understand what is really going on with the patient outside of the clinical environment. We also understood that the most valuable thing they have is the information from these patients when they are in the clinical environment. So we said, what if we took all this historical information from patients and many diseases and used the historical patterns to detect the same diseases earlier in other patients to help the patients get a diagnosis and to help the physicians provide more effective treatment? With this in mind, we decided to pivot.

José and I decided that the best option was to train ourselves to understand how we could analyse all this data to create a machine that would give you a probability of having a pathology. So, without overthinking it, José dived even deeper into the world of AI. I dedicated myself to creating relationships that would help us convince people of the importance of what we were trying to do.

Suddenly we found a disease that affected us a lot. It was malaria, a condition that kills an average of 700 children a day and affects the most vulnerable populations. We decided it was an excellent place to start and to try our application out. After a lot of effort, we began to see the light. Just at that time, one of the largest global pharmaceutical companies was looking for technology-based solutions that would help tackle the biggest challenges of malaria. We decided to apply. It was a huge challenge. We were competing with other established health companies and great scientists, researchers, and universities that had spent years analysing these diseases. However, as entrepreneurs, we knew that there is nothing to lose when you have nothing. And we decided to take a risk. Well, after many questions, forms, demonstrations and an interview with experts on the subject, we won the challenge, and we became great partners of this vast and fantastic entity.

Now we were no longer just young people trying to make change happen; we were already seeing a change. We cried with emotion, with joy to see that the efforts we had made – being far away from our families, feeling alone at many times – had started to pay off. This was the beginning of something entirely new for us. However, we were going through the biggest challenge that the world has gone through in my lifetime, a pandemic. That made us rethink what we were doing to help our home country, Colombia, with what we were developing. Our partnership with this great company opened the doors to build new relationships, optimize technology, and focus on bringing access to health to any place. We decided to gather information from many COVID-19 research centres worldwide to create models that would allow us to develop COVID-19 prognosis at a very early stage of the disease so that doctors would have the ability to make decisions in real-time, anywhere. We made it reality and put it into the field, along with our malaria-detection models. We took it to hospitals in remote areas in different states in Colombia. And, as it turned out, our models were unique. They started to generate word-of-mouth recommendations among many doctors, and we began to shape more of what Arkangel AI was at that time.

Arkangel AI is software that creates AI models to transform medical data into digital health solutions, automatically, without writing a line of code, and ten times more quickly than would otherwise be the case. It supports early diagnosis, giving results twenty times faster, is ten times more scalable, and five times more cost-effective, in increasing healthcare access. Today we have made over 25,000 detections in Colombia, and many of these in vulnerable communities. Maybe in a few months or years, what we do will be different in the way we analyse, test, improve and implement our solutions. However our ambition will remain the same, to help people live free of highly preventable diseases and to impact 100 million people in the next ten years, until the day when we can finally say that no one on earth will die from diseases that we can treat because they are not detected in time.

We have to say that the road has been a challenge, full of ups and downs, a road of thousands of questions and very few answers. However, our purpose has kept us focused. After these two outstanding achievements, we went through moments of much business and personal growth. We managed to grow our team; they are the magic of what we do in Arkangel AI today. We firmly believe, and in fact, José keeps repeating it: "Imagine if we can train our models with the best minds in the world, and bring this technology to areas where there is no access. We could change the way we provide healthcare, and we can generate a more equal system."

And this is precisely what we do in Arkangel AI. A simple idea to help our family became an opportunity to change people's lives, starting with our own lives. Almost two years after we started this journey, we must say that it is only the beginning. Indeed we still have a long way to run. The day will come when we will finally be able to say that no one on earth will die from preventable diseases. We, as entrepreneurs, build start-ups because we see huge gaps in the system. Problems that if we, together, don't solve, no one else will.

A Leap to Dream

Prakriti Bhandari (Nepal)

I still remember my voice resonating through the woods calling for my aunt, who had taken me along and left me in this unfamiliar place. The building was so huge, surrounded by the woods; I felt lost and cried my heart out. Little kids around my age looked at me with inquisitive eyes. Some of them were giggling while some adults were trying to comfort me. The situation seemed unfathomable for six-year-old me. But, without any other option, six-year-old me got by. This new place and new people soon became my new home and new family, where I spent my entire childhood and some of my teens.

In a mere word it was an orphanage, but for fifty of us it was a home. Our origins were scattered all over Nepal from east to west. However, our stories were similar. Most of us had lost parents, some of us had been rescued from the streets; everyone had poor financial standing. The significant fact was that we all needed love, support and a proper home. A proper home where we were safe, well nourished, loved and nurtured to become self-sufficient individuals.

Shangri-La Orphanage Home was established in 1998, with the objective of providing support to orphan children in Nepal, by Govinda Association, Germany. The initiative began by supporting 15 children but the support expanded, in December 2000, to 50 children when two houses were built in the south of Kathmandu Valley. The aim was ensuring the healthy and safe development of children in a natural environment. The development of the children was given the utmost care in the orphanage where we were encouraged and provided resources, for example to celebrate our own festivals. We had our own children's club with a democratic board where we were provided with a small fund, and the club decided unanimously to utilize it either for excursion visits or to organize events. The club had substantial responsibilities in the orphanage to plan the vacations, events and outings; to create schedules for cleaning and vegetable chopping for the kitchen; it also worked as a medium to communicate issues among us to the wardens. These responsibilities helped to build our leadership skills and a sense of responsibility.

Family, as we call it, cannot be confined to a biological tie. Family instils values within us, a sense of discernment which gives us our outlook on life. With all our diversity, but as a family, we shared a roof and an abundance of affection. We all had our own bitter and unique stories, but we were taught to embrace our story, so that we would never lose our connection with our roots. In those years, I was bestowed with values of compassion, kindness, empathy and a sense of unity. We were allowed to pave our own way following our passions, whether it was dance, sports or anything else. There were no boundaries. There is a distinct memory in my head where I asked to print a book which I wrote about "a frog that travelled to Germany", when I was in sixth grade. The very same week one hundred copies were printed. We never had constraints; we were allowed to leap to dream and make these dreams come to life.

I recall a New Year picnic in the woods. We saw an old homeless man lying helplessly on the ground near us. We asked our elders if we could give him some of our food. That day we ate only after we served him, and before leaving the place we served him again. In such ways, the seedlings of compassion in our heart were nurtured. Besides, there was a deeply embedded dream shared among us to serve the underprivileged and deprived. We understood that once we ourselves had been provided with an opportunity and benevolence in our vulnerable times, and as a result, in turn here we stood as civil, self-sufficient and compassionate human beings.

When I look back, I feel proud of our sense of community back then. I remember the road that led to our school was in very poor condition, with uneven stones scattered around and innumerable potholes in the middle of the road. In monsoon, the rain season, the condition always became perilous when we had to walk to school along this extremely muddy road ruining our shoes and sometimes even our dresses. At a time when even the local authorities ignored the situation, we not only bemoaned the condition but also gathered along with our schoolmates to repair the road. Picking up the garbage on the way to school once in a while became a custom. Even the smallest of our efforts in our school-going days bespoke our embedded compassion and the encouragement given by our elders to put our ideas into action, which nurtured this compassion even further. Unknowingly, we were freely providing our labours for the community. Despite everything, the bond among us children grew stronger and so did our voices. We never settled for others' ways, we had voices of our own. I remember us raising our voices for our own needs or else for each other. In this way, the relationship and unity among us only grew stronger.

Looking back, I recall us, the youth of Shangri-La Orphanage Home, gathering on a chilly November morning in 2014 to give our dream a substantial form. Some of us had graduated, but most of us were still in university. After three days of relentless workshops on the future of a group we had established called Shangri-La Development Association, we unanimously devised an abstract idea of working for the indigenous community known as Chepang on the outskirts of Kathmandu. The Chepangs have frequently been flagged as the "poorest of Nepal's poor". The very same day, we formed an Executive Board among ourselves, who would be the governing body of the organization, working voluntarily, and a team of employees, who would implement the activities, obtaining renumeration for their work. I was elected as the Secretary of the Executive Board of Shangri-La Development Association. We were driven on by our youthful exuberance and by the perpetual support of the compassionate people at Govinda Association, who had brought us up with such sensitivity, had graced us with values since our orphanage days, and were now building our strengths, guiding us away from our pitfalls and funding our projects.

The first step in our journey was Rapid Rural Appraisal. This is a recognized method used to quickly understand rural conditions, since it is very important to know the current demography, topography and problems of a place before starting planning for projects, and, most importantly, to plan projects that are compatible with the target area. I, representing the board, led the team of four employees and headed to a place called Kalikatar, Makwanpur. After six long hours of driving from Kathmandu, we were able to catch a bus along the bank of the river in Manahari. We were told it would take another two hours' bus ride to finally reach our destination. Only after the bus started did I become aware of the fact that it was a river bus ride. There were no roads – literally no roads. What they call a road is a river bank, where stones had been cleared by an excavator. The ride was extremely bumpy and there was a strong unpleasant odour inside the bus. Along the ride, I learned that this very same bus ride was the only way to connect our intended destination with the urban areas for "access", and the same ride was closed during monsoons due to swollen rivers. After two hours, we reached Kalikatar, Makwanpur. The place was so quiet, with few houses, surrounded by huge hills. We could constantly hear the babbling river. Now we were totally disconnected from the outside world. It felt like "living in the wild"; there was neither electricity nor a single network for telecommunications. We settled into our accommodation in a government building for the next few days. The night was so overwhelming, with mosquitoes and fleas. After this first day I was extremely disheartened.

The next three days were an average of eight hours a day of walking uphill with backpacks of instant noodles and cold drink bottles – and a stick for me, since I had little stamina for walking. These three days were full of staggering stories. There was only one secondary school for the whole area. Thus, the students desirous of getting a secondary education had to walk two to three hours every day to reach the school, while remote students with no alternative dropped out of school. Even this one school and the few primary schools had very limited resources, poor infrastructure and most of the times there were no teachers – all the result of poor governance by an unstable government. I felt highly privileged and blessed that day, having had easy access to a school with highly qualified teachers and abundant resources. But I also realized that I had the ability and opportunity to ease the local students' plight and that very moment I gained motivation to make a commitment and live by the dreams we had shared in the Shangri-La Orphanage.

Even daily survival seemed challenging there. I had

never seen houses so flimsy. They would typically have a thatched roof and were mostly one-roomed, with walls of weak sticks or dry corn stalks where air blew through and no privacy could be had. Every house was a shared space for cattle. Hygiene was a very low priority. Every family had an average of six children with very young mothers and poverty resulting in malnourished children. But, to my utter surprise, we saw a few churches made of bricks in the hills in a place where satisfying even basic means of survival was a struggle. I do not mean to comment one way or another on religious sentiments, but I saw "possibility" there and that was another motivation.

I saw infants left at home unattended, some of them sleeping on the edge of a rock totally by themselves. The landscape was so unfamiliar to me that I had a constant feeling of discomfort. The place was thronged with high, green, dome-shaped hills, circumvented by untamed and sparkling rivers. After the long walks in the humid weather, we would settle at the top of the hill and the panoramic scenery instantly settled our hearts amid the constant encounters and astounding stories, making us forget our discomfort. Well, there is a saying that every cloud has a silver lining. But the people settled in those high hills, with no access to vehicles and totally disconnected from the rapidly developing technologies, were grappling for even basic medical treatment. It would take hours to reach a medical centre and days to reach hospital. A place just a few miles away from the capital seemed alien to me. While politicians were muddling with power and befuddling with pretences of granting rights to people, people here were not even acquainted with their own fundamental rights, rights that the constitution promised to provide remedy for in case of any violations. It is inevitable that fellow nationals feel mutual responsibility to each other – and that was one more motivation for me.

On the very last day of our visit, we reached a village. The only school there was empty. We encountered very few people on the way and through some enquiries we learned that there was a wedding in the village and all the children had run away from school to witness the ceremony (and, as we assumed, to dig into the wedding feast). But we were perplexed to see a bunch of children and adults crowded around a speaker connected to a water battery, and the "feast" was small cartons of "Fatafat", instant noodles. Some of them were dancing, that was it. The groom was in everyday clothes and dead drunk with local alcohol. The bride was nowhere to be seen. I had never seen a wedding so small and pitiful. There was no ceremony; it seemed more like a public announcement.

When we were back in Kathmandu we took a deep breath and cheered. But later, contemplating those stories, I thought: "Those people were living such a laborious and tough life that we could not even live it for a few days."

With a few more visits for our baseline survey, and a few more workshops and meetings, we decided to work in three areas: Education and Empowerment, Health and Agriculture. Sustainability was a value we wanted to keep at the core of the projects.

In the area of education we, initially, took responsibility for fifteen girls who had to walk long distances and had to take risks in crossing rivers every day to reach school. We gave preference to Chepang children. The logic behind providing opportunity to girls specifically is that if they drop out of school, girls are more likely to get married and start a family. We hoped that by keeping them in a hostel and providing adequate resources we would be able to at least help them pass their school education, which meant that they would somehow be able to work and earn, they would not marry at such an early age and there would be less likelihood of malnourished children being born to young impoverished mothers. Providing hostel accommodation meant that a girl would not have to drop out of school just because of long school routes and the risks of crossing rivers on the way.

But we believed fifteen girls would be unlikely to have a big impact and that every child should be helped from a young age and should receive constant support so that they would not be disadvantaged in any way. Hence, we also supported four primary schools in the village, providing them with basic requirements such as whiteboards, desks and chairs. With increasing rates of dropout from school every year, we thought that a hot meal in school would attract students in the village, where most of the children were undernourished, and we decided to offer such support in all four schools. We also guaranteed to provide the students with a basic uniform and a bag, every year. And, crucially, we were involved in setting up a standard Early Child Development (ECD) class for pre-school children in every primary school. We also provided incentives to ECD teachers to work in the region and provided them with adequate resources, guidelines and training. We also set up a new secondary school.

Within our health project, we provided immediate first aid to villagers, and in critical cases we provided financial support for cases referred from the local health post. In addition, we kept track of the body mass index (BMI) of every child in the five schools and provided them with hand washing facilities and basic hygiene training. The fundamental objective of our health project was to increase medical support in pregnancy, in coordination with the Female Community Health Workers (FCHWs), since we found out in our baseline survey about high maternal and infant mortality rates and about the large number of malnourished children, due to low health literacy and low levels of sanitation and personal hygiene.

The agriculture project involved growing crops, producing fruits and vegetables by adopting Sloping Agricultural Land Technology (SALT), and practising animal husbandry. This project was intended as a demonstration to locals so that they could grow adequate food for themselves in their own land with different methods and techniques. Most importantly, we also intended to provide food to our schools from what we grew in the land. In fact, our projects were all implemented in interrelationship with each other so that they remained sustainable.

Another project we engaged in was Jumla Special Children Support (JSCP), where initially teaching support was provided to 35 Deaf children at Karnali Secondary School. We supported the children with educational necessities, like stationery, uniforms and other essential needs, and financed three teachers with deaf-friendly teaching skills. We have been giving support to Karnali School for Deaf Children since 2015. Today there are 40 children benefiting from the project.

However, we could not implement all the projects effectively, as a huge 7.8 Richter scale earthquake hit Nepal in April 2015, tearing down buildings, shattering significant cultural heritage and causing landslides and avalanches in hilly and mountain regions, thereby resulting in more than 8,000 fatalities and compelling 8 million people – one third of the population – to live in substandard temporary shelters with risk to life and health. The huge earthquake toppled school infrastructures, causing hefty destruction, with 5,003 schools in 14 districts damaged. This devastating earthquake also ingrained our minds with images of destruction and fatalities. The political blockade of the border to India exacerbated the situation even more. We in the Shangri-La Development Association were fortunate enough to survive the tragedy; however, among us, some lost their families, while some lost their homes.

Within a few days, the Shangri-La Development Association team gathered at the grounds of Shangri-La Orphanage Home and formed a new team, called Shangri-La Reconstruction Development Project, to carry out emergency aid activities with the funding support of Shangri-La Development Association and the Govinda Association. Everyone was working tirelessly day and night: some of us collecting relief materials we brought through the Indian border to Kathmandu and managing operations; some of us travelling to faraway districts to ensure affected families received support; while some of us were getting lost in administration and managerial work.

Personally, I went to an outlying region in Sindhupalchowk District, 330 kilometres north-west of Kathmandu, to distribute relief materials to nearly fifty families. The level of devastation was quite apparent there. The collapsed houses remained untouched. We could see the neon-coloured tarpaulins forming temporary tents hanging here and there, tents which were now a home to many. On the way to our destination, a bunch of people chased our vehicle, hoping for relief supplies – that would break my heart since we had another intended place to provide with relief instead. We had to leave the relief materials in military barracks since the destination had no access by road, and helicopter was the only way to get there. Shangri-La Reconstruction Development Project conducted emergency aid activities in 11 out of 14 affected districts with 55 tons of relief supplies, and reached 126 communities and 36,414 people within a month. In addition, a monsoon relief fund was made available to more than 5,000 people, providing temporary accommodation, and temporary learning centres for 2,500 school children and hygiene training for more than 600 people as well as medical care.

Tremors and aftershocks of the earthquake would return time and again, causing more despair. Many people were psychologically haunted after the tragedy. Everyone was forced to sleep under the open sky, for fear of earthquakes; even the Prime Minister's office was under tarpaulins. With the monsoon at our doorstep and a weak and slow response from government, there were warnings of a humanitarian crisis, especially in the rural parts of the country. The experience of this humanitarian crisis taught a lesson to the nation of the huge risks. This reinforced the understanding that the country needed to strengthen prompt crisis management, preparedness and planning infrastructures as the government, which was then struggling to overcome challenges and to respond to the cataclysmic events, now remains vigilant. Personally, I learned that, with cooperation and teamwork, any hurdles and difficulties can be passed through – and I am sure it laid another layer of patience in everyone.

The earthquake halted our project activities and our focus was diverted to the ongoing humanitarian crisis. We made sure relief materials were distributed to the affected families in Kalikatar, Makwanpur, too. The following years were full of challenges and hard work for Shangri-La Development Association. Within a few months, Shangri-La Development Association was immersed in comprehensive reconstruction projects such as the reconstruction of four schools and a literacy centre in Makwanpur, our School Building Reconstruction and Education Support Project (SBREP), as well as reconstruction of 36 houses in Makwanpur within our Shangri-La Reconstruction Development Project, in parallel with the regular activities of health, education and agriculture.

Our School Building Reconstruction and Education Support Projects were proposed immediately after the earthquake, even before the Government had established its Nepal Reconstruction Authority for the reconstruction of earthquake-damaged infrastructures. Maoists, who had taken over running the country in 2006, had mainly argued that the bureaucratic and centralized nature of the successive governments of Nepal had intensified inequalities and failed to meet the needs of the people. Therefore the transformation of Nepal from a unitary and monarchic country to a federal democratic and republican country from 2008 was one essential component of the new constitution and the government's delegation to the newly-formed provinces. The local government here in Kalikatar has included us in the development of the community here, especially in the areas of health, education and agriculture, since the earthquake. By 2020, Kalikatar had undergone a metamorphosis. Now, Kalikatar has Wi-Fi connection, a telecommunication network, and road networks to different villages, schools with substantially lower dropout rates and a better-equipped health post with standard birthing facilities. I would not say this is entirely the outcome of the presence of Shangri-La Development Association, but I would not hesitate to say that Shangri-La Development Association has had a huge role in all these. Today, Kalikatar has new governance with entirely new elected officials at the local level, covering a wider area and with a new vision for development.

We had never imagined our association would turn out to be so big. Even our smallest of efforts worked out so well. We feel blessed to have witnessed the paradigm shift that fell upon the lives of Chepangs and this place that was once so overlooked. We have gone through this transition with the communities of Kalikatar, through a humanitarian crisis, and their transition from poor living conditions where the government was not vigilant, to today when it has been transformed through the active local government, developing physical infrastructures and progressively developing social and economic aspects of the community.

I now understand the power of speaking up and making things happen. Even the smallest efforts to beget change in society can bring about substantial reforms; that is what we have learned over the years. We never in our wildest dreams thought our little efforts would have such significant impacts in the lives of the people. In 2014, when we committed ourselves to shape Shangri-La Development Association into a legitimate body, we were just a bunch of youths still in college or freshly graduated, with no professional experience. Nonetheless, the last six years have sharpened us through the experiences and challenges that came our way, and we ourselves have provided opportunities to other youth organizations, through outsourcing of construction activities or in the regular activities within the projects.

This is because we believe in the power of youth. When the abundance of energy and zeal of youth is unleashed, then there certainly will be significant impacts in development. In this way, active youth participation is a necessity in today's world, since it develops a sense of responsibility and ownership in community life. Youth should be involved in every decision-making process that concerns them, as this empowers them. When young people that belong to underprivileged and marginalized communities involve themselves actively in the decision-making process, they will have the opportunity to put a diversity of issues on the table, which will also allow them to have power and control over their own lives. In like manner, Shangri-La Development Association has also initiated the establishment of children's clubs in secondary schools and facilitates them to work on issues such as the environment around the school, supports them in organizing events and encourages active participation in the decision-making process on issues that affect them, which develops their leadership skills.

Contributing my six years to this organization has changed my life personally as well as professionally. Once every two weekends I, along with other board members, have been consistently working on decision making and planning for the organization, since most of us are busy on weekdays in our jobs or college. It has become part of our lives in some way. There are seven of us on the board. Two of us have government jobs, as a nurse and survey engineer, one of us has started their own business venture in travel and tourism, and one of us is working in an A-class banking institution. Personally, I have been enrolled in law school for the last five years, and graduated in autumn 2020.

After finishing my school education living in the orphanage, I was reunited with my relatives. The transition to getting along in the outside world was sometimes difficult, when I had to deal with everything that came my way by myself, and somehow I had control over my own life. Also, age brings responsibility and obligations and most difficult, you have to live by societal norms. At first I was constantly perplexed with the life in the community, a completely different world to the orphanage. It took time, but I adapted eventually.

I made it into the most expensive and renowned law school in the country, where most people come from well-off families and had been educated in the best schools in the country. Family status or a privileged life does not and should not indicate your standing in the future. I had an education in a medium-standard school, I was raised in an orphanage and I have spent most of my life trying to adapt to what came my way; only the support that I was given by Shangri-La Orphanage Home and the Govinda Association, both financially and in personal development, made me competent enough to settle my own future.

Today, I am the Secretary of Shangri-La Development Association and have recently graduated in law. I have done internships in the most renowned corporate law firm in the country and in the courts, under highly-qualified lawyers. I have myself facilitated human rights, women's rights and child rights training. And I have a great future lying ahead of me, which I see is a high privilege. With no concrete plans on the list, I want to engage in work that benefits people that are marginalized or deprived and stay in my own country, while there is a growing trend of young people flocking to foreign lands for work and education every single day. I know it is a huge decision to make for now amid an unstable political situation, an insecure social life, shrinking economy in this country and less opportunities within its boundaries. But there is always hope! In the aftermath of the huge humanitarian crisis brought by the earthquake, and the injured economy after the COVID-19 health crisis, it is time that we, the youth, have the audacity to unite ourselves to pool resources for the country and make our own efforts. And there is always hope!

Today when I look back, I love the stories I have lived, the impossible-made-possible history I was part of, and I avow my share in them. I feel highly privileged walking through it all, experiencing so many things: an unconventional childhood and painful stories, but also - and beyond anything else - perseverance. My experience through it all is hope in the dark, compassion that led to contentment, and the joy of comforting the one in need. I still have a long way to strive to serve the unprivileged, lift the marginalized and empower the excluded – a real uphill battle.

My Little Voice in Education

Wendi Njeri (Kenya)

Imagine growing up in a country where reading culture does not exist and nor is it encouraged. My name is Wendi Njeri; I am 16 and the founder of Books in Baskets Mini-libraries. I am sure you're wondering what Books in Baskets is and how a 16-year-old was able to start this. To tell you that I would have to take you back in time to where it all started. I am Kenyan and I live in the capital city, Nairobi; I've lived here my entire life. Life in the city of Nairobi was simpler back then, though this can be said of all childhood memories. I lived in a suburb built in the 1970's by the Commonwealth; it is about ten kilometres from the Central Business District. Most of the residents are lower middle-class. The houses, most of which are maisonettes, resemble a typical house in a British suburb with orange clay roofing tiles and white walls. This is where it all began.

I've been home-schooled since I was four years old, an experience which had its pros and cons. As a child the highlight of my days was walking around the estate waiting for my friends to come back from school to join in on the juvenile rendezvous. This went on until the Kenya National Library Service opened a library just across the street from where I lived. That library was the main catalyst in my journey to becoming a professional bookworm. I spent most afternoons, and all Saturdays, at the library, and when I couldn't be there physically I would have borrowed a stack of books to keep me busy. My interest and commitment to reading was recognized not only by my parents and friends, but also the staff at the library who awarded me a junior reader's prize at an event they held (though quite frankly the only things I remember from that event were that I got an award, books and I was on national television).

As I grew older my interest in books grew tremendously: I spent all my free time reading books, faster than my mom could buy or borrow them. I was on the nerdy side of the student spectrum; I tried to start book clubs with my neighbourhood friends but it was very frustrating because they either could not read all that well, didn't understand the book or had no interest at all. I'm very persistent, so I started lending (and losing) books from my home library to peers beyond my neighbourhood, and as time went by I realized that they were not interested, nor did they have any respect for books. My book-lending effort was rewarded by a cycle that went: lend, lose and argue. I still started many other book clubs and always ended up reading all by myself. Their lack of interest or ability to read always intrigued me, however my blind spot was my perception that school should provoke a sense of curiosity for reading in every child. I remember feeling like a scientist inquisitively watching their test subject in a lab through a glass.

Most adults around me would be fascinated by the number of books I could read willingly, outside of schoolwork. I vividly recall numerous arguments with my mother about bedtime, because when I started reading a book I only ever wanted to put it down once I was done with it. Most people thought I was an excessive reader but I believe that when someone is passionate about something it only looks crazy to everyone on the outside, but they are having the time of their life.

I never had the privilege of owning brand-new books; most of the books I owned were used books bought from resellers on the streets of Nairobi. Second-hand books collected and baled in Western countries are imported by business people who then resell these bales of books to street vendors. The vendors display the books on the street pavements and hawk the books to passers-by. It is the cheapest and easiest way to purchase a wide variety of books at a lower cost: one book will retail for the equivalent of €1 on the street but in a bookstore the same book will retail for about €8. Due to the lack of a reading culture, the bookstores only stock curricular books and bestselling book series for young readers. That's why I passionately advocate for donating old books; a book never gets old if you take care of it. Academic content never changes, it's just reprinted in updated editions.

Until I was a teenager, I never appreciated what reading widely had done for me. Academic work that was tedious for most students, like reading through extremely long and boring literature books and writing long essays, or analysing the contents of the book, became easier and manageable. Quizzes were a no-brainer, especially those that required a wide vocabulary knowledge. This marked the beginning of my participation in tedious extra-curricular contests, some of which involved essay writing, and expressing myself in different ways to a plethora of audiences. In my reading adventures, I had stumbled upon complex topics, for example geopolitics, advances in technology, business and various global issues, giving me the ability to actively participate in conversations that are typically in the adult domain. This sparked a confidence and curiosity that led to the discovery of an inquisitive side of myself, who enjoyed extensive research, with a bias to education.

While growing up, I had a guilty pleasure of listening to grievances about different education systems from students, parents, teachers and industry professionals. As I grew older I began to question a lot of the different methods of teaching that are currently available in education-delivery across the world. I continue to spend hours researching education globally and coming up with theories and solutions for how I would like to impact education, including inclusivity in education planning and generational change.

Education reforms should include our untapped resource of industry players from all sectors who lie in the elephant's graveyard as far as education reforms, planning and execution are concerned. Professionals in the education sector are doing their best, but it is folly to always trust the biased eye, instead of consulting the view of outsiders to give the best possible outcome, making use of a fresh set of eyes to re-examine what the last group might have missed. Small changes in industry must swiftly be accommodated in our curriculum, but this will only work if we change our perspective on learning resources, utilizing the traditional textbooks but also incorporating current affairs, media, and the internet and work experience as resources in learning at all levels. This will expand the learner's perspective from the now to the future. This will give education an appeal to the Millennial, Generation-Z and Generation-Alpha student, who is in a fast-changing world and deserves a dynamic curriculum. A curriculum that quickly captures the progression of petrol cars to electric cars, pills to vaccines and human workforce to robotic workforce, for instance.

The first time I was asked how I would want to make a difference in my community was during a career guidance session as I transitioned to high school, and my answer was crystal clear: education. I was given a challenge to write it out and implement it at my level with the resources that I had available. My first idea was quite simplistic: finish high school and literally donate my entire home library to a school. Voilà! The more I voiced my idea to different groups of people, and got positive feedback to go ahead and implement it, the more the need affected me on a different level.

The Kenyan school system is a blend of private and government-sponsored schools. Government-sponsored schools are scarce and overcrowded. These schools are supposedly free but charge miscellaneous fees for exams, sports etc. Working with government schools would give me the challenge of the bureaucracy of dealing with education officers, who can be corrupt and biased. Since public teachers are transferred from one school to another, continuity and finding people to take ownership of change would be difficult. This is a challenge I will take up sometime in the future.

Private schools are further classified into well-endowed private schools mainly found in urban areas, and a vast majority of private schools which are owned by entrepreneurs in education, seeking to meet the gap left by the few government-sponsored schools available. These schools' facilities are dictated by the amount of school fees the entrepreneurs are able to raise, but more often than not these are just classrooms, textbooks and teachers. Schools like these in marginalized communities are my main target. Through my interactions with adults and potential partners, the inequality of the systems in Kenya became more apparent. I became conscious of the challenges of corruption, bureaucracy and discrimination based on my age that I would face on this journey to make my vision a reality. It immediately became less about donating my home library and more about implementing long-lasting change. I realized that donating to one school does nothing for the bigger picture because in as much as the students would benefit from it, how many more still need this resource?

This insight was the jet fuel to the beginning of my project and my journey in impacting education. I consolidated all my ideas into Books in Baskets Mini-libraries, a library project whose vision is to provide books to school-going children in Kenya who have no or limited access to a library. My goal is to use books to inspire the children and open their minds to a world beyond their circumstances and locality. I designed a community-centred system that would ensure students have access to reading materials with minimal logistical hindrances of library constructions, overwhelming catalogues and staffing. In order to make the implementation as efficient as possible, I identify a local contact to act as a patron for the mini-library, I liaise with the host community to provide a room, and together we build basic wooden bookshelves for the storage of the books. I acquire baskets from the local community and colour code the books and baskets based on reading levels. The baskets are used to ferry the books to and from the storage area during reading sessions in classrooms and homesteads.

I have established two mini-libraries so far, each with a book count of 1,500 books, accessible to the students in the host school and the community at large. The books in the library are mainly non-curricular English books, however I donate any books that are in good condition. I decided to focus on supplementary books rather than textbooks and other curricular books that are already provided by the government. The set-up for each mini-library costs approximately $2,000. This includes the cost of building bookshelves, renovating the storage area, purchasing of additional books to give the library a good balance of book genres, and other miscellaneous costs, like courier charges for sending the books to the libraries or stationery and stickers to mark the books. The patrons of these two mini-libraries are members of the community who have chosen to run privately-owned schools as their way of giving back to their communities.

I have received touching stories of how the libraries have impacted the community. Students are becoming more engaged learners, reading and researching freely in the library. The schools have recorded increased student enrolment and learner engagement during class time and reading sessions. One story in particular stood out to me. It was from a university student who benefited from the library. He needed a specific book to study for his end of semester exams. Normally this would have meant a trip to the capital city, Nairobi, causing the sacrifice of time and money. Fortunately he was able to find the book he needed at the library. This report really stuck with me because it made the impact very tangible and encouraged me to continue with my dream. A great contrast from the stories that were told to me about how students used packaging papers from grocery items like flour as extra reading materials. Their textbooks are locked away in school, leaving them with nothing to read. The opportunity I had to explore and understand the world through books is now a reality for these students. Finally I am connecting the need with my purpose and vision.

This success has not been without its challenges. My inexperience has been put to the test, as I continue to learn on the job. Working with limited resources has both tested my values and instilled new ones. I vividly recall the physical challenges I encountered during the setup of my first library, the funniest one being an unexpected rainstorm that revealed a leaking roof on the eve of the library launch, minutes after completing the final setup. I had to hurriedly transfer books from one corner of the room to the other in questionable lighting, since it was dusk, and deep in the countryside, with no electricity. I then rose at dawn the next morning to reset the library again, and host the community eagerly awaiting the launch of the very first library in an 80-kilometre radius.

Another challenge has been balancing the project and my school work. At first they both stalled, during the 2020 coronavirus lockdown situation. As soon as life started to open back up, I began to learn how to plan and schedule for both my school work and my project. Sometimes I do get carried away with one – my passion wins most of the time, but I still find a way of getting back on course with my studies.

In my lifetime I would like to see libraries established in schools across Africa, and a reading culture beyond curricular textbooks inculcated. In the next five years I would like to grow Books in Baskets to a national scale with at least 60 mini-libraries. Kenya is divided into 47 counties each with a local government; I hope to have at least one library in each of these counties among marginalized communities. I hope to perfect and tailor-make the Books in Baskets library model through adaptability to the specific communities, and have a model that can be replicated across Africa. Increasing partnerships and networking will create a seamless network of book collection centres and volunteer networks to support the growing activities. I receive some books that are in a bad state. I want to make Books in Baskets more eco-friendly by using origami art to recycle these books, teaching the library beneficiaries soft art skills, and using the art to bring light and colour into their classrooms.

As I transition into my university years, I would like to build networks and gain experience on how to better myself in my role within Books in Baskets, interact with education systems across the globe and eventually join the policy makers as an industry consultant. Books in Baskets is my little voice in education, an echo that will be audible one day across the African continent.

Are You Willing to be Small? Finding direction amid self-doubt and chaos

Jonathan Chu (Malaysia)

What is a "Joyplace"?

I spent the last eight years focusing on one thing – turning workplaces into Joyplaces. A workplace becomes a Joyplace only when the business is thriving, and the people are winning – there is growth, satisfaction, and fulfilment. This, as you can already tell, sounds like an ideal, something that is almost impossible to achieve. You're not wrong; I once thought that myself too. But I also told myself that the greatest things that shaped this world were once thought impossible. Yet, someone did them. One of the leaders I've always admired for shaping the world through innovative thinking was Steve Jobs. Yes, he led with an iron fist –

which I do not agree with – but I admired the audacity that led him to create Apple. Where audacity is concerned, I'm nowhere near Steve Job's capability, but I would like to consider that my efforts are still changing lives and, by extension, the world.

I work as a consultant specializing in corporate culture and people. In my eight years of designing and deploying corporate culture transformation projects, I have met many leaders who struggle with the thought of "treating employees well". An example is a restaurant chain that I worked with.

In Malaysia, being a waiter is not a respected job. That is why not many locals would choose to be a waiter, if they can help it. As a result, many restaurants have no choice but to resort to hiring non-Malaysians. Visas are difficult and expensive to process, and workers are paid low wages so that restaurants can maintain low operational costs.

There is also a trust deficit between restaurant owners and workers. Because wages are low, workers typically hop jobs at the sign of higher pay. Owners are not only frustrated that the visa they paid for is now not bringing any return, but they also now have to process new visas and conduct training all over again. Service is disrupted and customer experience is negatively impacted. Existing staff need to fill in the gap by working harder for longer hours. Naturally, they begin looking elsewhere to get more pay to justify the work. As you can tell, it's a vicious cycle.

This restaurant chain that I worked with experienced the same challenges. To discourage their non-local workers from leaving, they withheld their passports. To keep the company running well and afloat, they directed all their attention to operations such that they had no energy to look into the living conditions they provided for their employees. When we spoke with the workers, we found out that they had to take turns to sleep on flea-infested beds as they were working from 9 am to 11:30 pm every day, and no one was home to clean the house. They also had to walk through dangerous neighbourhoods just to get to work. We also found out that there had been instances where restaurant managers were immensely stressed and that they resorted to shouting at their workers, some to the point of verbally abusing them.

When we spoke to the leaders of the restaurant chain, we learned that they were under different pressures and these details had slipped through their fingers. That was when we found ourselves drawing their attention to their vision of delighting customers and explaining to them the importance of delighting their *internal* customers first before their external ones. As we worked with the top leadership of the company, the defining moment was when the CEO finally spoke these words: "I need to treat my employees well so that they know what 'delighting others' means. That is how they learn to treat our customers well!"

"Yes!" I leapt with joy! "You get it!" This may seem obvious to an outsider who is not hard pressed to deliver results, but for the CEO, his leadership team and mid-managers, this was a blind spot.

The majority of companies are less than joyful places. For them, either the business is not thriving or the people aren't winning, and I'm here to change that narrative. Having said that, I have not always had that clarity. I fundamentally believe that the best teachers don't provide answers, but questions or statements that spur deep reflection. In fact, it took a long, painful journey for me to finally embrace this vision – turning workplaces into Joyplaces.

The Anchoring Question

It was a summer afternoon in 2014. I was seated in the middle of a park in Innsbruck, a city in Austria. Around the city were mountains, and I was choosing which one I'd like to take a quick hike. One hour later, I was hiking one of them, my back to the city. I turned around to see how far I'd come. My eyes scanned the scenery, and I spotted the park I had been in an hour ago: a small square, now appearing smaller than my palm.

I was just a speck of dust an hour ago, came the dawning realization. I spent a good ten minutes staring into the distance, allowing myself to soak in the sight, the gentle wind caressing my face, ruffling my hair. All of a sudden, this question came to me – *'Are you willing to be small?'*

I considered that question.

Small.

The first reaction I had to it was distaste. Who'd want to be small? Nobody wakes up wanting to be small. If anything, people would be more likely to begin their day wanting to be great. Now, *great* has a nice ring to it. But it's loaded with expectations. Ever since I was young, I had always wanted to be great, but I'd never defined what 'great' meant. In my mind, when one was great, one was celebrated. And I wanted to be celebrated – as a person, and in everything that I did. But what I didn't realize was that every celebrated person is known to be great for *something*, either a skill or an achievement. So, what did I want to be great at? I never had an answer. When the question "Are you willing to be small?" came, my knee-jerk reaction was confoundedness. I stood on the same spot, my gaze still locked on the park in the middle of Innsbruck, as I allowed the question to simmer.

Are you willing to be small?

As I moved through life, this question has never left me. In fact, it became one of the anchors in my life. I began developing a relationship with the word 'small'. Today, being 'great' means being 'small' to me. They are no longer opposites, but synonymous.

The Pivot

My company made a 180-degree pivot in 2015. Originally a training academy for the advertising industry in Asia, my company had been seeing a downward trend in revenue. When we spoke to our clients, we realized that they had to take on twice the number of projects to achieve the same amount of income, and could no longer afford to send their people for training.

We had to decide. Do we continue, or do we change? The core team stared at one of the whiteboards in our meeting room. On it were notes of pivot ideas, pros and cons, and the challenges ahead of us if we were to continue. The atmosphere was serious and sombre. The idea of pivoting was scary, as we were the market leader in Malaysia and a strong contender in Asia. Pivoting meant discarding everything and building from the ground up. Could we succeed?

Would we succeed? What prices would we, as individuals, need to pay? Were we ready for that?

Finally, our CEO bit the bullet: "The facts are clear – either we pivot, or we die. It's as simple as that. Let's focus on corporate culture." We spent the next few hours unpacking why focusing on corporate culture was the best way forward. Many of our graduates had big dreams and hearts. They left our programmes ready to raise the game in their organizations and be the change they desired to see. Some wanted to improve their company's working environment; some wanted to raise the quality of work they provide to their clients. Some wanted to create more inclusivity, transparency, and diversity in their companies; others wanted to change the way their leaders negotiated contracts with their clients. Despite the wonderful intentions, many gave up. Some experienced burnout, some became jaded.

Based on our conversations with our graduates, we discovered that there was little that individuals could achieve in their organization if they did not secure the buy-in of their leaders, peers and subordinates. When it comes to change – even if it's for the better – resistance is often the first thing that we slam into. If we do not have other people on board with change, there is a high chance of burning out and giving up.

We had no control over how effective our graduates could be in securing supporters. So, instead of building individuals who would find the odds were against them in the face of championing change at their workplace, why not go to the root of the problem?

Culture drives every organization, no matter the size. Shaped through leadership, it is how every company functions. It dictates how decisions are made, what gets rewarded, and what gets punished. It decides what gets recognition and what doesn't. It determines the capability and quality of execution, and drives all organizational strategy. Quite often a culture has evolved organically as a company grew and the management team are unconscious of it or even of the possibility that things could be different. Because of its pervasiveness, it is arguably the most difficult thing to change in an organization. For example, how do we create greater inclusivity and diversity in companies? How do we change the narrative and help companies realize that work-life balance is critical for the longevity of the company well-being? We need to address the corporate culture, because the existing culture has dictated how things function, the people they hire, and the biases that come in the way. Doing so means going to leaders who are open and ready for change, and supporting them to create the organization they envisage. This would also mean that our graduates would get to focus on being the cheerleader of change and not worry about securing buy-in from others.

Another reason for making this pivot was the impact it brought. Instead of spending our resources and impacting individuals, we could channel our resources to impact organizations. Secure a company as a client, and we'd be able to reach out to thousands. That was impact exponentially magnified. Looking at the potential of impact gave us goosebumps. It scared us. For many of my team, this wasn't their cup of tea. So they left. In two weeks, only four people remained. That's a very small team.

But being small enabled us to be more nimble and agile. It also meant fewer stakeholders involved when making decisions, fewer differing perspectives, and less noise. This did not negate the pain of seeing comrades with whom we had built good working relationships go. Furthermore, existing clients still had to be managed; bread and butter work had to continue to keep us afloat. We found ourselves working longer hours than usual. But change was bigger; our eyes were fixed on it. Sometimes, the way to achieve a dream is to let go of the success of the past and start small. It is scary, but necessary.

How do you turn workplaces into Joyplaces? You start small, and you start with your team. Find ways to treat them well, because when you do that, you're not just contributing to them as individuals, but to their families as well. When individuals leave work, they return to their families. As much as we can insist on separating work and personal life, everyone only has a limited amount of energy every day. All of us have little energy (and patience) for those we love after a long, hard day. They don't get the best of us, but our work and clients do. How is that fair?

Humans are wired to love and be loved. If our families don't get the best of us, it is only natural that they'll find it elsewhere. Sometimes people resort to distractions, some end up choosing the wrong friends. Some escape through work, some develop bad habits. Mental well-being suffers, self-worth deteriorates, and disempowering beliefs are picked up that come in the way of personal effectiveness. No wonder there are so many breakdowns in our societies! Now, I know that this can sound over-dramatic. I am cognizant that there are other factors at play too – which I readily admit – but one cannot deny the importance family plays in every individual's life.

The quest to turn workplaces into Joyplaces is so critical because every workplace – regardless what the work is – takes away the best of people. Often, people are returned to their families in a tired, worn out state. If we preach about making this world a better place, we should start with companies. People spend at least one-third of their lives working, which takes the best of them every day. If joy is not what they walk away with at the end of every working day, it is their families and ultimately, they themselves and the work that suffer. We need to change that narrative.

With this as our cornerstone, we began knocking on doors, looking for clients to work with. I still remember our first meeting. It was with a lady who had possibly come from a bad meeting. There was no hint of a smile on her face. She was cold, distant. "Why should I trust that you can do good work?" she asked. I felt really small. Starting something new meant beginning with being small and *being seen* to be small. This was humbling – and necessary. Just like many things in life, if you knock on doors often enough, if you share the same message with the same level of conviction enough, one day someone might finally answer the call with a 'yes'. In 2016, I finally secured our first client. After that, the subsequent rejections no longer stung as much. In 2017, we secured another large client. In 2018, the same thing happened. Along the way, many other smaller clients came along to work with us. Soon, we found ourselves in a place of fewer rejections, and more acceptance.

If we hadn't started small, this wouldn't be part of my company's story. In fact, I might have left the declining company and joined another one. I wouldn't have understood what it meant to hold on to a vision that is bigger than myself. When my initial team started leaving, I did wonder if I was making the right choice. With 20-20 hindsight, I am grateful that I hung on.

Are you willing to be small? That question now has a different meaning to me.

Faithful to the Little

I wanted to do great things. In my mind, greatness looked like celebration, my face on magazine and newspaper covers, and people contacting me to congratulate me. But I learned that true greatness looks more like love. It is not something we receive but give. Only when people experience our love, do they celebrate us. That's when we become great in their world.

In 2014, I received a text from a participant in one of our training programmes explaining that she was afraid, and that she had been barred from entering Malaysia. For context, this participant, I'll call her Renee, was part of a 3-month programme that I was leading. This programme helped individuals to transit into advertising by equipping them with strategic and creative skills. In between every module (which was a month long), Renee would exit and re-enter the country so that she could be in Malaysia with a tourist visa. However, the third module was five weeks long, and she had to leave the country after the fourth week. When she tried re-entering Malaysia, she was stopped by immigration.

Prior to her leaving Malaysia, we had ensured all the necessary paperwork was in place. In my mind, there was nothing immigration could do to put her in a dangerous position. I also bore in mind that she was not a criminal, nor had she been involved in any criminal activities. *She'll be fine*, I thought to myself.

We exchanged a few text messages, and the last message I received from her was, "They put me in a waiting room."

"You have done everything right. You have the papers. You did not illegally leave the country. You followed the protocol, and you have not done anything wrong. There is nothing they can do to you, Renee. You'll be fine." That was my reply. I waited for a while and received no reply. Thinking that all was under control, I called it a night.

The next morning, I texted my CEO to inform her of this situation. Within an instant of hearing the news, my CEO exploded with rage – and this was when I "woke up" and learned a very important lesson about leadership and putting people first. "Can you imagine how terrible she must have felt? A small woman in front of burly immigration officers, without her passport, and with nowhere to go?" asked my CEO, outraged. "You should have told me immediately. I would have dropped everything, driven to the airport, and made sure that they released her immediately. How would you feel if that was your sister?"

That last question brought it home, like a slap on the face. The pain set in, and I immediately saw that this was beyond having the right papers. It was about standing up for someone who needed me. It was about being a leader who cares.

The Japanese have a saying: "Everything is a rumour until it flows through your veins." I thought I stood for leadership, but evidently, I did not. The true definition of leadership escaped me, and was only a rumour to me as it did not flow through my veins. It didn't cross my mind to *deeply* consider what Renee was feeling, and this was a wake-up call. My CEO was right – I *should* have informed the team immediately, dropped everything, and gone to rescue Renee. It was the right thing to do, and I failed her for not responding that way.

Leadership is about the small things. I grew up admiring world and business leaders. I remember thinking to myself when I was a child – when I grow up, I want to be like them. It had not occurred to me that leadership was about the small details and doing the small things, no matter how apparently insignificant.

If I couldn't even be there for one person whom I knew by name in her time of need, I had no business wanting to change the world. My dad's words rang true in my mind: "Charity begins at home. If you can't be faithful to the little things, you won't be faithful to the big ones." Maybe that was why the question "Are you willing to be small?" hit me like train moving at a thousand miles per hour.

Renee was released. Her passport, documents, and belongings were given back to her. She was not harmed. As for me, I walked away forever remembering this exchange. While I was grateful Renee was unharmed, I learned that leadership was about making seemingly small but important choices. Choosing to deeply care for others, choosing to be empathetic, and choosing to put others before oneself, tuning in to what they might need, and being there for them. It was about doing what is right, not what is easy.

Difficult situations put us in a state where our values are truly tested. We get to experience what it is like to be in a dilemma. Often, these situations do not present themselves in a grand fashion. They are often small decisions we have to make. If we make the right choice, we know that we have lived according to our values. If not, we get to take a cold, hard look at ourselves and honestly answer these questions – *What went wrong? What do I stand for? How does that apply in this situation?*

I decided I would like to start making better choices.

Hiking the Mountain

When my company made its pivot in 2015, the market was not ready for the conversation on corporate culture. That changed very quickly. By 2018, our clientele had tripled and the revenue doubled. The team grew from four to 32 people, and we found ourselves consulting for companies beyond Malaysia. We also started winning awards from regional award shows, and other companies started knocking on our doors to form partnerships. Additionally, our clients saw the value of our work and were walking advertisements for us. We also developed a "Joy Audit" that informed companies how close they were to becoming a Joyplace.

Did our clients become more of a Joyplace? We'd like to think so.

Remember the restaurant chain company I told you about? They revamped their HR policies. They no longer withhold passports, they bought new mattresses and made sure there was enough for all staff, and they also hired buses to safely transport their employees. Managers who did not know how to handle stress were given workshops on stress management. Employee engagement shot up and customer engagement increased too. The journey wasn't simple. My team had to take each leader aside for numerous difficult conversations and coaching sessions. We had to guide them to let go of their old ways of working and consider new methods of engaging their staff. The process was slow, but we had to be the lighthouse of what treating others with love and kindness looks like in the workplace. This slow guidance eventually bore fruit – not only did employees feel more respected and heard at the workplace, the business picked up and began seeing increasing profits and productivity too. In other words, the workplace began to slowly become a Joyplace.

That said, the best stories are not the ones reflected in income statements or presentation decks, but the ones that are told in corridors. Let me tell you about someone I will call Ainah. Coming from an underprivileged family, Ainah worked in an insurance company, which had been our client for 12 months. Her only job was to ensure all guests, top management, and the board of directors got hot tea when they attended meetings. In Malaysia, it is a custom to offer finger food and beverages in meetings as a sign of togetherness and hospitality.

One fine day, one of the directors observed that the tea she made was delicious, and this was her response: "Just like you protect our clients through insurance, I protect you by making sure the tea you drink is not only the best, at the right temperature, but with the least amount of sugar." (Malaysians customarily like their tea sweet.) "Only when you are healthy can you serve our clients." That was how she saw her role as a tea lady in serving their clients. That's ownership. How often do we see non-executive staff having the capability to articulate the purpose of their work and align it with the company's?

Let me tell you another story. Marvin (name changed for anonymity), who used to work in a training company, had worked his way up from a humble background. He was rough around the edges, but took great pride in his work. In one of the training sessions, a participant accidentally dropped her phone into the toilet. Flustered, she exited the toilet without flushing and asked her friends for help. Without a second thought, Marvin stepped in and told her and her friends to prevent people from entering the ladies. Swiftly, he went in, retrieved the phone, sanitized it, and returned it to the owner. When the team asked why he chose to take such an action, this was his response: "I am part of a team that upholds excellence; I don't want to let you down. I want to be excellent too." That is the power of corporate culture. Get it right, and the rest will take care of itself.

Along the way, we collected small heroic stories like these, and one thing was consistent: When leaders begin on their journey of turning their workplaces into Joyplaces, a mindset shift happens in their companies. People begin to focus on the right things. Work gets done, and people get to go home with more energy. As a result, they have richer relationships, and they find life more fulfilling. This creates a positive loop, as the externalities positively impact the work at the office too. Our work is far from done, and we don't intend to stop any time soon.

Be the Change

In 2010, I led a nation-wide survey that posed this main question: "What do you think the Malaysian government can do better?" More than 20,000 individuals responded with suggestions on improvements they desired to see in education, entrepreneurship, economics, society and politics. When we followed up with the question, "What have you done about your suggestions?" only about 100 people reported having started a project, initiative or start-up to solve the challenges they cited. This was alarming.

Many have much to say about how broken systems are, but how many are open to be the solution? In my work, I have met countless individuals commenting about how un-joyful their workplace is, and when I asked about what they are doing to improve the experience of the teams – not companies – a common answer I get is: "Why try, when I can't affect change?" What's shocking is, many times these answers come from social enterprises and non-profit organizations!

In my eight years of working with companies, I learned that building companies is akin to parenting. Every parent has principles upon which his or her parenting style is built. These principles guide the way ground rules are set and engagement with children is conducted. Growing up, each person observed his or her parents and decided they will be the same or completely different from their parents. That can be said about being a leader too. We pick up our leadership principles from our previous employers. Just like how I picked up the importance of putting each person under my care before my comfort. You will have your examples too. Some of them could be great, but some may not. Here are a few examples: "Don't train your employees too much, lest they find another job." "Either step up or step out of the company." "I don't expect all my staff to be high performers; I just need them to do what they're paid to do." I'm sure you can think of more examples. The cold, hard truth is: these principles transcend industry or sector. That is why we find less-than-joyful workplaces everywhere; and that is why building Joyplaces is so critical.

Three years ago, I was invited to speak to an audience of entrepreneurs. There were about 200 of them, all wide-eyed, inquisitive, and hungry to learn how to build better organizations. One of the participants raised his hand and asked, "How do I get my team to care about my business more?" "You don't," I answered him flatly. I proceeded to explain that leaders oftentimes expect their people to go above and beyond, but rarely ask themselves the question if *they* have gone above and beyond for their people. Have we, as leaders, built the organization we desire to see?

Have we done our utmost to help our employees build a life they desire to see for themselves? Have we given them access to the opportunities, growth, and mentorship that they need to thrive? Have we helped them see a bigger, better, smarter version of themselves – such that when they come to work, they realize that they're not working for us, but for themselves and their loved ones? Have we built an environment that honours their heritage, background, race, traditions, and families? Do we respect them with our words, actions, and behaviours? If we want to create a world that has more dignity, inclusivity, diversity, compassion, and love, we start with our teams, before demanding that of our companies and nations. Our circle of influence is our platform to create the kind of world we desire to see, and demonstrate that it is possible. If we struggle with the small team we already have, imagine how difficult it would be on an organizational or national level. Let's start with more action, and fewer judgments.

Fortunately, just as parents are more self-aware nowadays, business leaders are the same too. Many are humble enough to take a cold, hard look at themselves to ask the difficult questions. Some, whom I've personally known, even go to the extent to over-compensate their staff. Sometimes, even though the intention of being a great leader was there, it did not create the desired impact. This is why my heart beats with compassion for leaders who try.

As a leader, we are marked by our intention, the results we create, and the perception others have of us. I have met many leaders whose hearts were in the right place, who pumped in resources to turn their companies around, and who did their utmost best to create the Joyplace as they saw fit. However, not all their efforts were met with appreciation.

Being a leader is tough in today's world. Many judgments about our actions and behaviours are hurled at us. In so many ways, we may fall short in the eyes of others. It is not for lack of trying, I am certain. So this is what I want to say: Keep trying. Keep trying to find your voice in this noisy world. Keep declaring your vision about how much better this world can be, and keep inviting different viewpoints to challenge your perspective. Keep going at it, and soon, you will find yourself surrounded by people with whom your message resonates.

Just like Barack Obama said, "We are the change we are waiting for." Let us continue to build the Joyplaces we desire to see in this world.

What's Your Mountain?

By now, you can tell that I have several things that I hold close to my heart. The first, the metaphorical mountain I aim to conquer: to turn workplaces into Joyplaces. The second, the mindset I need to have to succeed: Are you willing to be small? The third, the anchor to take action: making better choices. I am still letting life unravel what it has in store for me, but what anchors me the most is the second – *Are you willing to be small?* If you have people around you, are you willing to do the small things to put them first? If you are the leader of a company, are you willing to look into the small details that would differentiate between a workplace and a Joyplace? In this context, being small is being great. Let us dedicate our attention to even the littlest of things.

I continue to hike my figurative mountain. I hope that one day, there'll be more Joyplaces than workplaces. One day, we no longer need to dread Monday but look forward to it as a start of the week that brings opportunities to create, to grow, and to be satisfied with the work we are capable of doing. So, I leave you with these questions, in the hope that they will spur some reflection: What is your mountain? What would you like to achieve? What are your dreams, hopes and visions for yourself, your loved ones, and your world? Are you willing to be small? To do the different things? The things that seem insignificant? Are you willing to pay close attention to the people around you, who may not help you achieve your big dreams, but will challenge your personal values and decisions? Are you willing to make better choices, based on the vision you have and your willingness to do the small but difficult things? May these questions illuminate your way forward, as you put one foot in front of the other, and scale your mountain. All the best!

Future Economics: Showing how economic growth can be more just

Marjorie Atuhurra (Uganda)

When a child is born it's a time for family celebrations. That's true around the world, and especially in Uganda, where the whole community shares in the joyous welcoming of the new arrival. But it wasn't true in my case. I was the child of two schoolchildren. My mother was 14 and my father was only two years older. I was never accorded parental love. I was named a bastard and an evil child by my family. I grew up at the mercy of whoever cared to take care of a vulnerable and unloved child.

I was raped at the age of ten. At this time, I was staying with my paternal aunt and she, together with her husband, had adopted a boy who was then close to 20 years old. We were left at home alone, and he used this chance to enter my room and forced himself on me. He later told me never to speak up and because I was terrified I never told even my aunt when she came back home. This torture affected me then and until today I am still nursing those wounds.

By 15 I was on the verge of being sent for a child marriage myself. I had not even had my first period. I was very unaware and scared of what the future would bring. Then, at age 19, I got pregnant and gave birth to my daughter at 20 years of age. Only then did I find people who genuinely wanted to help me and my baby.

The Social Innovation Academy, for short SINA, is a place that turns stories and experiences of marginalized youth into opportunities for social entrepreneurship. I was told about SINA by a family friend, who told me to apply as a facilitator trainee. It is at this place that I turned my sorrow and pain into an opportunity to empower and change the lives of girls and women – some of whom had suffered even worse experiences than I had.

Five years ago, I created my own organization, the Gejja Women Foundation, where we envision a generation of well-educated, economically independent, and self-determined women and girls who are in control of their own bodies and lives and can stand up for their rights. Uganda has one of the youngest populations in the world. Three-quarters of the population lives in rural areas, with limited access to economic opportunities and depending heavily on agriculture, like growing subsistence foodstuff and rearing animals. High gender inequality and poverty limit the chances of women and girls to receive an education or engage in formal employment, leaving them to do most of the unpaid domestic labour. As an NGO, Gejja focuses on economic, educational and social empowerment as a fundamental driver for change.

We have four main projects. Firstly, we have the education support that is rendered to those young girls who cannot afford to stay in school, but would wish to continue with education. Secondly, we practice permaculture[8] in schools and communities to promote increased financial independence for rural women and to boost the nutrition of schoolchildren, especially in government-aided schools. This also enables mothers to offer balanced diets to their families. The surplus produced can be sold to buy supplies for the schoolchildren, such as books, pens and sanitary materials. Thirdly, we create business opportunities for rural women through the Gejja Women Centre. Through our mentoring and coaching process we empower women to start up their own businesses. These social enterprises can benefit not

---

[8] Permaculture is an ethics- and design-based process used to make agriculture more sustainable, restore soil, conserve water, and redirect waste streams. The process is inspired by the everyday relationships found in nature.

only them but also the society where they are living and the environment at large. The fourth big issue we are tackling is menstruation. Our programme "Safe Girl" focuses on safe and comfortable menstruation through the production of re-usable sanitary pads.

We started with 35 women and are currently working with over 3,000. Some of our beneficiaries were school drops-out on the verge of being sent for early marriage. With the help that we got from small donations, we managed to send them back to school. We have empowered 350 women through business and development programmes. These are rural women starting their own enterprises, such as restaurants, merchandise shops, craft-making, wine-making or candle-making. For example, Natukunda Florence started her own restaurant to benefit the community around her and also earn an income for self-sustainability. Her business is growing well and she is able to support her family. She no longer begs others for money. Such a restaurant is important in the community because most of the working-class or middle-income earners don't have time to prepare food, especially the university students who attend an institute in our community. These people are regular customers to the women's businesses.

Since March 2020, 45 women have benefited from our seed loan project. We anticipate growing our seed-growing project by 15 per cent by 2022. The seed loan programme started in March 2020 after Uganda went into lockdown. We started with five women, to whom we gave vegetables seeds to plant in their gardens under our supervision. After three months they harvested their produce, sold some and used some as food at home. We have continued with this programme to support more female farmers who have access to land for agriculture but might lack the tools, seeds, and fertilizers. We at Gejja give them the seeds and all the required equipment and at the end of the season they sell their produce and bring back 15 per cent of the profits to the foundation to finance further projects.

Menstruation is one of the most difficult issues worldwide, not only in Uganda. Even in developed countries, menstruation is one thing that is not easily talked about. When it comes to Africa, it is an even more difficult topic. Children are never given ideas about what to expect when they start their menstruation. They use filthy material including banana fibres, banana leaves, polythene or toilet paper during their menstruation. At Gejja Women Foundation, we believe that menstruation should never isolate, shame or oppress any woman or girl. We have reached 100,000 girls through our menstrual hygiene campaigns and produced 50,000 Safe Girl reusable pads that help to keep schoolgirls in class. For many adolescent girls, puberty is the most vulnerable time of their lives. It is estimated that 65 per cent of Ugandan females, and 78 per cent across East Africa cannot afford to finish their education and are therefore denied decent employment. Of these girls, 60 per cent drop out of school and 47 per cent have unplanned pregnancies. HIV prevalence among girls is four times that of boys.

At Gejja Women Foundation we believe that when women are educated and empowered, they can be great agents of transformation in their communities, impacting not only themselves, but their families and their environments. If economic growth is to be just, then we need to give better opportunities to young women like my 14-year-old mother and the little girl that she wasn't allowed to love.

With a Little Support, Someone Can Go Far

Jovita S. Mlay (Tanzania)

I thank God for his graces. I am married and a mother of three children, with a grandson. I have a bachelor's degree of Commerce in Accounting, and a master's in International Trade, both from the University of Dar es Salaam, Tanzania. I worked as a public servant, as a financial management officer, from 1988 to 1996. Then I joined the Civil Society sector in 1997, engaging in business and advocacy work to promote women's and girls' rights through a non-governmental organization known as the Tanzania Gender Networking Programme (TGNP). TGNP works locally, nationally and internationally to advance gender equality and a transformative feminist agenda. Through TGNP I was motivated to do more on economic empowerment for women and girls. Thus, in 2010 I established SASA Foundation with eight other like-minded individuals. SASA Foundation aims to enhance the productive capacity and inclusion of women, children and other marginalized groups into socio-economic systems from family and community to national levels, to contribute towards economic growth and poverty reduction in Tanzania. We see a future for impoverished families and individuals, particularly women, children and persons with disabilities, achieving well-being and a sustainable social economic status.

As of today, SASA Foundation has successfully mobilized and facilitated the organization of more than 70 women's groups amid marginalized communities and disabled women in the regions of Tanzania. We educate them on gender (social transformation), human/women's/ children's rights and microfinance. We also facilitate development of income-generating activities as well as reduction of the work burden (care work) on young mothers to enable them to engage effectively in productive roles. Through this, there has been noticeable achievement by individual women and groups in terms of improved welfare, education and health of family members, especially their children.

Beginning SASA Foundation

My experience with Tanzania Gender Networking

Programme (TGNP) in 1999 enhanced my knowledge of women's issues, children's rights, marginalization and inequalities in societies, which are rarely discussed. Being an accountant for eight years I had no chance to engage with different types of people to discuss such issues. The accountancy work limited my knowledge to financial matters without relating the work to peoples' lives.

However, since my childhood, I had strong feelings and instincts about women's lives. Whenever I came across a woman suffering, whether I knew her or not, I would sympathize, and interrogated my soul as to whether I wanted to be married. I felt marriage, as I saw it around me, was a punishment that I could not associate with. I used to quarrel with boys who tried to force a girl to do anything; most of the time I got angry with such boys and even men. However, I associated with boys when studying, especially in secondary school and university.

Most of the time I would ask myself, "Why is a woman disadvantaged?" I grew up with that notion, until I started working, and met and got married to a man that I found a bit different. He listened to me, he gave me space to present issues of my interest and together unified our arguments throughout our friendship – and now as a wife and a husband.

As I got out of the Ministry of Finance (MOF), one of the female commissioners in the Ministry of Finance (who observed my character) talked to me and said, "Jovita, I see you have feelings on women's life and marginalization issues because most of the time when we meet, you keep on raising concerns about women's freedom in the workplace and women's role at the family level, while the husbands in the office do not show any concerns for care work." She then said, "You should join this organization, the Tanzania Gender Networking Programme." She added, "It is a very credible organization that provides space to discuss women's issues and inequalities." I agreed with her and went to find the organization (TGNP). Every Wednesday the TGNP ran an open seminar where everyone with an interest could go to listen, learn and share her or his thoughts freely. I liked the platform and made it my plan to participate at least twice in every month as I was interested in the discussions and deliberations of each seminar. After a few months the management of that organization asked me if I would like to be trained as a Gender Trainer. I accepted and I managed to go through the training programmes: I am now a Trainer in Gender and Trade. Switching from accountancy work to social work was not very smooth, but with practice and enthusiasm I became a good trainer. The challenge was to adapt to look at the different nuances and perspectives on a situation rather than applying the black and white principles I used in accounting.

I think because of my background as an accountant, whenever I conducted gender training, I was more aware of the practical phenomenon of women and poverty than of social discrimination. That led my concerns specifically towards women's economic empowerment, all along, in my gender trainings and hence led me to the idea of establishing SASA Foundation. I am still a member and a board member of TGNP. Through it, I work mostly nationally and globally. However, I go directly to women through SASA, to facilitate women to amplify their voices in unity (women's economic groups) and in movements at the local level as they demand change to oppressive and unresponsive systems and structures. These systems and structures hinder them from cultivating their potentials as employees, businesswomen and investors to transform their individual, family and community lives.

Before I moved into establishing SASA Foundation, I started mobilizing my relatives, especially my husband, brothers- and sisters-in-laws, friends and potential individuals. Out of those, four men and six women accepted and we joined forces to put SASA into place. I asked those who accepted if we could start a basket fund, where we would be contributing to support disadvantaged children in our villages. We analysed the situation and found one of the main problems was the number of kids in need of support because they had lost parents due to HIV/AIDs. They were orphans living with their grandmothers. A few of them lived with their mothers only, as a result of early pregnancies (young women got pregnant and were rejected by the men who were responsible). The idea was accepted and we implemented it in four villages in Moshi district and one village in Longido district.

We identified primary schools where we could have teachers identify the most vulnerable children (MVC), to whom we distributed school materials and welfare items depending on what was contributed. The schools that benefited from the programme were Kilema/Kisuluni in Moshi and Sinya Primary school in Longido. We then went further, identifying children in the villages to support, depending on what we had collected. In doing that exercise, we came up with the idea of establishing our own system to reach needy children. We mobilized women's groups, who were responsible for identifying MVC and contacting us for action. This was also thanks to my mother-in-law, Ms Salome Sabas, who mobilized women in the neighbourhood and influenced the women members to start a credit scheme for themselves, to use the scheme for economic empowerment. This women's group, that started with seventeen members, was involved in identifying MVC in the village to let us look for ways to help the children in education and general welfare.

As we continued with our programme to support children, we realized that the guardians, especially the grandmothers and widows, lived in a very harsh environment. The contributions we could make were minimal and thus we were able to support only one child in a family. That disturbed us as the members of the family where the child was living were left in the same environment of hardship. The child that received the support continued with the same situation. The child needed more than just educational materials, but we were unable to provide.

Establishment of the Women's Empowerment Programme

I, in collaboration with my colleagues, realized that supporting a child only educationally does not give much benefit to the child nor the family. Therefore we devised and adopted my mother-in-law's system of mobilizing women in a village or locality to organize and engage in discussion on what hinders them to progress economically and socially. Despite the fact that everyone wanted a micro-credit scheme at the beginning, we encouraged them to first understand their context. We trained them on social transformation through developing an understanding of gender inequalities and the role of a woman in creating socio-economic justice in their society. Thus, the training was followed by establishing a credit scheme and grants for women to engage in productive activities and to support the most marginalized grandmothers and widows respectively. In doing that, we came up with the idea of forming SASA Foundation in 2006, which later in 2013 was registered as a non-governmental organization. Some members had no interest in running an NGO, but they were willing to contribute in case we needed financial resources to support any marginalized child. Given that I was leading the process, I automatically become the Executive Director of SASA and have been since then.

Putting SASA Foundation into action

The name of SASA Foundation started way back before we thought of formalizing it. As mentioned earlier, SASA originated as we engaged in an educational programme for MVC in Moshi district and later in Longido district. We managed an education fund that was contributed by Charley and Joan, a couple from the United States of America, for MVC for four years and that made a very good impact in the Maasai community by having 68 children enrolled in primary education and 33 in vocational education.

In due course, after registering SASA, we continued

with educational support through women's economic empowerment in these two districts, with an addition of three other districts, namely Arusha district (Arusha region), Hai (Kilimanjaro region) and Babati (Manyara region). Our approach was to create links and collaboration with religious institutions and local government to ensure continuity even when we were not there. In doing that, we established potential relationships with government officials, such that when they had gender related challenges with a community they invited SASA to support, even where we had not established a programme. In addition, our collaboration with religious leaders had a great influence as religious leaders of a particular area, especially in Longido and Babati, become effective gender equality champions. However, it needed lot of training and practical examples to have religious leaders, especially from Roman Catholic and Muslim backgrounds, understand the benefit of the gender equality concept. It was very hard on our side to accommodate the rigidity of those leaders, even though one of them was the initiator who invited SASA to operate in the region.

A priest (Rev Fr Pius Shao) contacted me to establish a women's economic empowerment programme in Enduiment as he observed women in that area, particularly Maasai, were oppressed, discriminated against and facing serious violence. He also told us that girls were married forcefully under the age of 15, and hence getting access to education was a nightmare for a Maasai girl. He therefore appealed to SASA to help in promoting women's economic empowerment and access to education for girls. He put it clearly that even the church was facing challenges operating in such an environment.

What amazed us at SASA during training sessions for women (developing their conceptual understanding of gender and the importance of gender equality in development processes) was that the priest argued that women cannot be equal with men in many ways. He raised his comments in a few training sessions that he participated in. However, as we deepened our analysis of gender relations and the change of women and men's perspectives in a given time, he slowly came to agree – though with reservations sometimes. He then became our ally and ambassador to translate these messages to the community through his preaching.

We succeeded very quickly in organizing more than 600 women into economic groups in Enduiment and engaged in remarkable economic activities with women who previously could not get out of their homes as the husbands would not allow it. As of now, the women monitor violence against girl children and fellow women. They have become entrenched into community leadership and own a big storehouse that is used by community members to store their harvest (grains). The economic groups of about 30 to 40 members were facilitated to form an umbrella group with the name WAMSOE (meaning Women Let's Move Ahead). SASA trained the leaders of small groups and facilitated them to form an effective secretariat, which helps SASA to monitor the groups and run our Saving and Credit Scheme (table banking) so efficiently.

Since 2012, the secretariat of WAMSOE has been

trained by SASA to manage a small fund for the credit scheme that was initiated by SASA to facilitate loans to individual women and groups, while all members were trained in gender and business skills. The individual women borrowed from 50,000 Tanzanian Shillings (TZS) to 2 million TZS to establish or expand their businesses. Mostly they carried out businesses including horticultural farming (tomatoes, Irish potatoes, peas and onions), poultry and cow/pig keeping. Some of them did trading in maize and beans or clothes, or ran saloons and small shops. Some groups borrowed up to 4 million TZS to buy and sell maize as a group, run a milling machine and make tourist products (mainly Maasai jewellery). Success is seen in the increased confidence of the women; some dared to contest in community leadership elections and took representational positions. Many of them sent their children to secondary school and colleges for further studies. SASA has extended support to grant-giving to older and very poor women as well as giving employment to the children who were supported in tertiary education by their mothers (members of WAMSOE). Many women were attracted by the idea of transforming their homes, and more than 20 women have changed their mud houses into good modern brick houses. WAMSOE is running a bank account that was initialized by SASA Foundation in 2015.

Elsewhere, in Moshi District at Kawawa Road and Kilema juu Wards, more than 80 women were mobilized and organized into groups and trained in gender, business skills, technical farming and processing of milk and vegetables. They were supported with storage facilities and seed money to establish a fund for a saving and credit scheme. Here, we see evidence of the way those women transformed their lives, especially in education for their children, housing and even with a multiplier effect, as men in Kawawa Road requested to join the women's groups, having seen the progress on the women's side.

Another manifested success at Kawawa Road was in women making the shift from hazardous work to safer work. Three women were doing stone-crushing while watching their babies around the mining area, but two of them have left and now have a maize business, having got a loan to buy maize in bulk and sell it in the market. The leadership of Kawawa group is very effective as they applied the knowledge obtained from training in business skills: their loan system is very clear and well documented in a register book. That system and the achievements by the women moved the villagers, particularly men, to establish their own revolving fund while others requested to join the women's groups.

More work on women's economic empowerment is seen in the Arusha District around the SASA office, and in Nduruma. The women around the SASA office have capitalized on their proximity to the office in such a way that they carry out table banking (revolving fund) at the SASA office every Friday and apply to SASA to get quick information on legal matters. They have gone beyond economic issues to addressing violence against women, girls and boys in the localities. That happened as SASA trained the women in women's and children rights and then went further to form a team of paralegals, which keeps an eye on incidences of violence. A number of incidences, especially girl child rape cases and early marriage and pregnancies (schoolchildren, especially during COVID-19) were brought to the SASA office and others before they were brought to court.

I witnessed a number of achievements made by women, because I am regularly invited to groups towards the end of the year when they are dividing their profit (a kind of dividend) to members to celebrate Christmas and New Year. The groups in Kawawa and Longido (WAMSOE) had been sending a gift to me as appreciation of what SASA has done for them. But when they give me money I return it back to their basket as my personal contribution.

The Kawawa women's groups faced a major obstacle between 2016 and 2020, due to the closure of the Kilimanjaro Cooperative Bank (KCB) on political grounds. The women could not access their money to give loans to those who needed money to engage in farming. They really suffered. I personally went to the government offices at the Department of Community Development to ask for support so that the women could get their money back to continue with their businesses. They only got 300,000 TZS, which was just enough for a loan to one person. So the whole of that period they really operated in difficult circumstances. But we could not do much, because we did not have a project for that. Only at a private level, you can give 200,000 TZS to someone who is really in a dire situation. I offered my own money, just so they could use it for survival.

Other Benefits

Maasai families normally have very small houses that are constructed by women. Our mission at SASA Foundation was also to facilitate the women of Longido to address issues of settlements and children's right to housing as children were not considered to have a suitable place to sleep. In addition, many families sell their farm produce immediately after harvest – when prices are at their lowest – because of limited space for storage. We therefore induced discussion for the groups to acquire a plot to build a storage facility. The first mission is succeeding slowly for many of them as few have gone fast in building better homes. The women solicited a plot from the village leaders and got about a quarter of an acre and luckily a lady (a tourist) from Switzerland who visited the area got interested after hearing the story of WAMSOE and funded the building of a granary for the women. The storehouse or granary is currently used by community members (women's group members and non-members) to store their maize and beans to wait for an appropriate time to sell them. The granary building has a big office room which is rented for social activities like weddings and meetings in the village. There is another room used by the women as an office.

In Hai District SASA managed to support widows through a cattle-keeping project. We visited a village called Nkuu Machame, as we were invited by one of the women activists there to help her organize and support widows. We identified the most vulnerable and granted two cows to two women. Besides granting cows, we trained them, to make them feel energized and empowered to engage in economic activities. During the training, the women said to us: "We have so many problems, and thus we are not sure if we can work together without fighting." Based on the training they came up with a cow project, which we were able to buy. The widows preferred a man as their leader as they felt weak by themselves. The man coordinated the project and the members' activities. Their group is called TAKIMA. After a year they invited us to see their achievements. We were amazed as we found that one of the two had started building a house. We asked the woman, "What did you do with the cow?" She said, "After getting the calf, I started using the manure in my small plot to plant vegetables and sell them to neighbours as well as supply them to nearby markets. With the manure from the calf, I planted and harvested vegetables continuously and thus I have money every day." She went on narrating the way she spent the money from the sale of vegetables. She said, "So the first weeks of sale I thought of buying cement to renovate my small hut. Somebody said: 'Don't do this. Why don't you start a small house with two rooms with this cement, as you are buying it little by little? We will get someone who will do construction whenever you have money.'" She concluded, "As a result, with a push from my colleagues, our leaders and our trustee (the lady who invited us), I managed to start the house." The male leader and the trustee told us that everyone was encouraging the woman because her husband died of HIV. She was so desperate as she thought she would die soon and leave her kids with nothing. The neighbours supported her to fetch water for the construction. Now she is in that house. We therefore concluded that activating self-actualization helps to cultivate determination, and hence with a little support, someone can go far.

Disability Projects

In the course of reaching MVC and MVW in communities, we learned that girl children with disabilities in poor localities and remote areas have no access to education. Their care is also challenging given the economic condition and weak livelihood of their families. We revised our mission, to include advocacy for inclusive education. SASA Foundation received a little support from the Ecumenical Disability Advocacy Network (EDAN), which operates globally with a focal organization in Nairobi (Kenya) to advance advocacy work focusing on gender and disability inclusion. We started with sensitization of government officers at district and ward levels who deal with social welfare and community development, as well as officers in charge of early and primary education. We extended the sensitization programme to Arusha (Arusha, Meru, Monduli and Longido districts), Kilimanjaro (Moshi Rural and Municipal districts) and Manyara (Babati district).

On the other hand, SASA reached out to women with disabilities through the women's economic empowerment. With support from EDAN we enrolled women with disabilities in income-generating activities. In Babati we facilitated 21 women with physical disabilities to engage in tailoring and they formed a group of their own to run a revolving fund. The group has not improved much, due to limited resources to monitor and backstop their operations and manage the fund. That is because SASA has not been able to raise funds to rollover the project as Babati is far from Arusha, and hence more resources are required to be able to travel regularly to Babati or deploy a focal person to manage day-to-day operations. The programme to support women and children with disabilities at Babati was backed by the Galapo Roman Catholic Church where the priest in charge was very cooperative and provided a venue for disabled persons to conduct meetings once in a month. But the meetings need supervision and support to ensure women with disabilities participate and raise issues accordingly. In addition, the meetings do not take place if there is no new agenda or facilitator, which we think is because they have not strengthened their unity. They need more training in leadership and support to be able to carry out advocacy, especially on inclusive or special education for their children and other issues.

Besides advocacy for inclusive and special education for children with disabilities, and support to women with disabilities, since 2018, SASA provides humanitarian support to the most vulnerable families (MVF) by distributing essential needs such as food, soap and clothes. The needs of those families are overwhelming because if any of the parents in a family is disabled or a child is disabled, then the manpower of such a family to engage in productive activities is very much constrained. Social protection systems in Tanzania have not been very effective. SASA has mainstreamed the issue of disabilities in women's economic empowerment though not much has been done due to limited resources, as mentioned earlier.

Early in 2019 the president of the African Initiative (AI)[9] visited SASA Foundation to see what we do and promised to work with us to focus on persons with disabilities. Since then SASA participated in a number of meetings, with invitations from AI to share our success stories and our approach, but unfortunately the intricacies of coronavirus wiped out our expectations of AI support. In order to carry out advocacy on disability inclusion, one has to conduct surveys to determine extent of the problem. As such, SASA expected to work with AI to explore gender concerns within disabilities and establish potential mechanisms to address gender inequalities and exclusion due to disabilities in Babati, Longido and any other area that would be determined through the survey.

However, we do have success stories based on advocacy for inclusive education in Babati. A girl with serious physical disabilities in Babati completed primary education and was selected to join secondary education. But she could not go as the school that she was allocated had no facilities for her. She could complete the primary education because the school was nearby and her parents and siblings supported her to go and come back with a specialized bicycle. A district education officer called at SASA to ask for support. SASA took the initiative to contact the higher authority of the Ministry of Education to raise concern for the disabled girl. Initially we thought of looking for financial

---

[9] African Initiative was an NGO supporting some of the most vulnerable women and girls in Tanzania through local programmes, operational from 1997 to 2021.

resources to accommodate her in a boarding school, but found it hard to do it as it was an emergency. So we kept on pushing the top ministry official until the matter got attention. The regional and district offices were ordered to ensure the girl gets allocated a school immediately. The regional leaders took up the matter and started renovating the toilet in a school that was identified for the girl to be in boarding. Our work to monitor whether the girl got into the school stopped when the schools closed because of COVID-19 in March 2020. The mother called us to thank us for the initiative and care, but she emphasized that we should push them so that they complete the renovation. We gave her hope that we will follow up, though it is hard for us as an outsider to push government while the work is in progress. Advocacy work needs diplomatic moves rather than force, especially for an action concerning an individual.

Establishment of Daycare Service to Reduce Care Work Burden in Low-Income Communities

We realized, thanks to our Women's Economic Empowerment (WEE) Programme, that there was a need for a daycare service to free up the time of young mothers to engage in economic activity to better their financial situation. Providing this service would also help us ensure the children were being well cared for and would give us an opportunity to provide education and empowerment to the young women that we might not otherwise have access to. We got funding for training from the Women's Fund Tanzania (WTF) so that some of the more mature women in the community who had more time could provide the daycare service. We now run eight daycare centres and have also established partnerships with other organizations that run daycare centres. The centres also provide outreach services into the community to help these young mothers as well as anyone else who the local women's organization has identified as being in need of support. Some of the girls that we have helped to educate also gain work experience in the childcare centres.

Paralegal Training

Again under our WEE programme, women came up with concerns about violence against women and children. Some members of the groups failed to participate effectively in the groups' activities due to domestic violence. Many times cases were brought to us but we were unable to handle them all. Therefore, SASA, in collaboration with Inherit Your Rights and Project Abroad Tanzania trained a few members of women groups and SASA staff on human and women's/children's rights. The trained women formed a team of paralegals. With a paralegal team that is aware of women's and children's rights we are able to discuss and handle simple cases related to women in domestic violence and child rape, though the cases need further processes in court and healthcare. SASA organizes women's groups to observe the proceedings and trends of the cases that we have submitted before court. The observation task has been very hard as a case can be postponed so many times without any justifiable reason, and hence there are increased costs to monitoring a case, especially when we don't have funds for transport and media.

SASA Foundation also collaborates with other organizations and the local government in the districts that we operate in to advance legal aid to women, children and persons with disabilities. We have formed a network of organizations in Arusha known as Arusha Legal Aid Network. The purpose of the Network is to work in coalition and advocacy, on human rights focusing on women, children and persons with disabilities, in collaboration with national organizations and networks of like mind. My role in the network is to lead on a gender agenda, given SASA's expertise in transformative feminism as well as resource mobilization to ensure growth of the women's movement.

Operations with Coronavirus Crisis

COVID-19 has made our work complicated and hard. SASA has tried to support the most vulnerable families as well as provide education to safeguard the lives of women and their families.

Educating and supporting women to ensure they adhere to rules of social distancing, washing/sanitizing hands regularly and wearing masks in a crowd was our main activity, as the majority of women's groups that we deal with do business in local markets that are always full of multitudes of people. We became very conscious of the women in markets. I live near a big market that brings in more than 5,000 people as customers and sellers of different items. In that market there was not any rule that was applied. When I asked some women whom I know as members of groups why they were not taking any measures even after training, they quickly responded that there were no facilities, especially water and buckets. However, the reasons given were the same, even after we supported them with buckets and soaps/sanitizers. The challenge of water and logistics and how to monitor the process of washing and interactions was difficult as there was no structure or organization, such as a one-way system for customers or any fixed selling points. The women told us that they could not buy water for washing as they were not able to sell their tomatoes and vegetables even at 500 TZS, because the sellers had flooded the market more than the buyers. They said that every individual was coming to take their chance at a livelihood as other workplaces like hotels were closed and social activities were banned.

The women went on asking why they should fear an unknown disease more than the hunger which a family might suffer from not going to the market. They tried to identify the number of cases they had heard of and concluded that no one cared even if you contracted COVID-19, nor bothered when you died of hunger. They said, "Life must go on. If one has no food she can't think of washing hands and so on. All she will think of is food for the children who are home because of school closure."

The problem concerning children and the COVID-19 crisis is more that of poor infrastructure to facilitate equitable access to education, information and protection against violence and abuse of any sort. The measure that was taken to avoid spread of COVID-19 to school children was to close schools. Some introduced online teaching. But many of the children in our villages missed the opportunity due to lack of internet facilities. Some of the schools in remote areas introduced a system of sending homework through community leaders, but that was not teaching. So they kept on assessing children throughout, without teaching or giving them a learning opportunity except for those in town and families that could afford internet.

As well as this, children were left to themselves at home with minimal protection and care, as their mothers were almost all out earning a livelihood. We observed children roaming around in groups as if there was no coronavirus problem. We questioned ourselves and the women's group leaders as well as community leaders on whether we should do something. We mobilized women to address the problem of children walking around aimlessly. SASA could also take some children from the daycare centres to stay with them throughout, to provide full protection to our children. Because of limited resources in SASA, I took some kids and they stayed with me in my home.

With support from Women Fund Tanzania and a few individuals, particularly our previous volunteers including Johanna (German), Alexandria (Italian), Chiara (German), Jonas and Annina from VOICE (German), and Barakah (Swiss) we were able to reach about 126 families to provide food and were able to provide protection materials like buckets and sanitizer/soap for public areas, mainly in local markets.

We also trained women's groups to follow up on their neighbours and act collectively on incidences of

COVID-19. We facilitated SMS groups for women (who could not afford internet or WhatsApp messages) to text regularly to wish everyone well-being and reduce the impact of self-isolation and marginalization. The text messages were also targeted to protect children who were home as the schools were closed. The students had nothing to do at home, especially those who could not do studies online, and this thus made girls and boys roam around, and many of the teenagers ended up in uncontrolled sexual situations. SASA tried to follow up on women to monitor the students' movements and share with the parents to ensure all children who were out and about were accounted for. Our role at SASA was to call the women leaders and ask if the members of groups were interacting and keeping in touch with their neighbours. We also received names of those who could not afford meals and found ways to support them. We also educated each other when there was a coronavirus case in a family to ensure the rules were known to them.

Sustainability of SASA and Making an Impact

We are thankful to Women Fund Tanzania, who made SASA foundation visible, as well as raising my profile as an individual. As a result of this visibility, I have been invited to make presentations on the women's movement in Arusha, and occasionally been a Guest of Honour or Keynote Speaker at important meetings or women's day celebrations. For example in 2020 I was invited and honoured to be a Keynote Speaker at the UN Court in Arusha at women's day celebrations. The keynote speech was particularly intended to present the work of SASA Foundation and challenges faced in realizing women's rights. Personally, I now also work as a consultant on gender, where I have had an opportunity to conduct analysis of various policies and programmes relating to Trade, Sexual and Reproductive Health, Workers Unions and Gender Barometer in Tanzania.

My hope is to have SASA establish its own centre and make use of the knowledge that we have been gathering to run the organization with a social entrepreneurial attitude. I trust that we will find a partner to collaborate and make the organization grow, and become an institute and a hub for Women's Business and a Child Development Centre. Why combine a Women's Business Centre and a Child Development Centre? It is because I don't feel comfortable when I see a very successful woman without attaching her success to an impact or legacy that she has left behind. That is to cultivate something. This is our ambition.

Co-Creating the Dreams of Underserved Communities

Aravinth Panch (Sri Lanka)

A lot of people don't know exactly when the conflict between Sinhalese and Sri Lankan Tamils started. The systemic oppression of minorities by the majority had been on the rise since Sri Lanka got independence in 1948. There were attacks and retaliations from both sides. According to public records, LTTE (Liberation Tigers of Tamil Eelam) attacked the Sri Lankan Army in July 1983. In reaction to that, anti-Tamil rioting started in Colombo, the capital of Sri Lanka, and then spread to other parts of the country. Over seven days, Sinhalese mobs attacked, burned, looted, and killed Tamil targets. Estimates of the death toll range between 400 and 3,000, and 150,000 people became homeless. Around 8,000 homes and 5,000 shops were destroyed, leading to an estimated economic cost of US$300 million. Sri Lankan Tamils fled to other countries in the ensuing years, and a large number of Tamil youth joined various militant groups. This series of events is known as Black July and is generally seen as the start of the Sri Lankan civil war.

There were curfews and military round-ups by the army that started happening frequently in 1984. The situation was getting worse, especially for young men from Tamil communities. My mom's family consisted of five boys and two girls; my youngest uncle, Jeyan, was 19 years old at that time. One of my mom's aunties had lived in India since 1960, and my grandfather decided to send Uncle Jeyan to her in Chidambaram, India, to keep him safe. In November 1985, my uncle Jeyan, accompanied by another uncle, Kamalan, travelled to Colombo to fly to Chennai, India. My Uncle Kamalan carefully sent off his younger brother and was returning from Colombo to Batticaloa by bus, which is more than 330 kilometres and several hours of travel through deep forests. Near to Polonnaruwa forest – close to the border between Sinhalese and Tamil regions – Sinhalese armed forces stopped the bus. They chose specifically educated and physically well-built Tamil men to get out of the bus, including my Uncle Kamalan. All eight of them were taken to the forest and mercilessly shot.

My mom's family was frightened that Uncle Kamalan didn't come home two days after his trip to Colombo. So my grandfather, my other uncle, Karunai, and a family friend from the Muslim community – familiar with the area around Polonnaruwa forest – borrowed a vehicle and travelled to the forest searching for my missing Uncle Kamalan. When they reached the region, at the Tamil side of the forest, they were stopped by an unidentified armed person. He asked them to get out of the van because he wanted to take the vehicle for himself. My grandfather was in the driver's seat, and he didn't want to give up the vehicle. If this vehicle was lost, he wouldn't be able to pay for it, because he was a public bus driver from a low-income family. So he decided to escape the situation with the vehicle by starting the engine, but the gunman ruthlessly shot everyone with his AK-47. The accelerating vehicle hit a roadside tree. My grandfather, in the driver's seat, was killed by a bullet in the head; my Uncle Karunai, sitting behind, got a bullet partially in the head, and others were injured and unconscious.

A few days later, Uncle Kamalan's body was sent home by the army, in a closed coffin with a note saying that unknown forces had shot him and the family was not allowed to see his face as it had degraded in the forest. Grandfather's body was sent from the hospital, again with a note saying that unknown forces had shot him. However, a secret apology message was sent from the LTTE stating that it was a careless act of an LTTE cadre who wanted to take the vehicle from my grandfather forcefully and acted thoughtlessly. A beautiful innocent family collapsed in a couple of days. They were neither supporting nor opposing the LTTE or the army, so they became collateral damage to this violent civil war, like thousands of other families in Sri Lanka.

After the death of my grandfather and uncle, many of our relatives escaped Sri Lanka. They emigrated to countries such as Canada, the UK, Germany, France, Switzerland, Denmark, Norway and many other countries in the Global North. However, my grandmother, who faced the terrible experience of seeing her dead husband and son, decided not to go anywhere. My mother is the eldest daughter; therefore, she chose to stay in Sri Lanka, which is why my story continued in Sri Lanka. However, my father moved to Saudi Arabia to work as an electrical engineer after my elder brother was born in 1981.

Similar to many other civil wars around the world, another challenge during this civil war was that there was not only one group of rebels. LTTE was the dominant group, but all the groups had conflicts with each other and killed each other. The so-called freedom fight was divided even within itself. The conflict was breaking out into a full-fledged war. We started hearing many stories from our relatives and friends about their villages being wiped out by the army as retaliation for the attacks by the LTTE.

I learned from world history that other countries very often exploit such internal conflicts to gain geopolitical dominance. I believe that was one of the reasons that India decided to send a military intervention to Sri Lanka. According to public reports and my personal encounters with several Indian officials who were part of this story, India was clearly involved in Sri Lanka since early 1980 by arming, funding and training the LTTE in southern and northern India. After talks with President J. R. Jayewardene of Sri Lanka, in 1987, Prime Minister Rajiv Gandhi of India signed the Indo-Sri Lanka Accord to give power to the Tamil-majority areas and designate Tamil as an official language of Sri Lanka. Indian Peace Keeping Forces (IPKF) to Sri Lanka were initially not expected to be involved in any significant combat. However, within a few months, IPKF started fighting LTTE in the northern province, especially after the death of 17 LTTE prisoners, including two area commanders in the custody of the Sri Lankan Army. IPKF launched several combat operations to destroy the LTTE-led insurgency, and the IPKF committed numerous civilian massacres and rapes during the conflict. In my opinion, the IPKF played a vital role in extending this conflict into a second decade. The LTTE decided to take revenge because they believed Rajiv Gandhi and India had betrayed Sri Lankan Tamils. So they sent a group of suicide bombers to India in 1991 who assassinated Rajiv Gandhi and 57 other people. In my opinion, this incident is the reason the Indian government and people have hated Sri Lankan Tamils since then.

After the IPKF left in 1990, Batticaloa came under the complete control and influence of the LTTE. My father came back to Sri Lanka from Saudi Arabia when I was three years old, and this was the first time my father met me. Many families in the conflict zone didn't have any educated young men living with them because they were targeted and killed by the army or forced by the LTTE to support their operations. During that time, my father was taken into custody by the LTTE to provide them money, gold or any valuable material because he was working in Saudi Arabia. After that incident, my father left the country for many years. Growing up without a father was never a problem for me as a child because it was the same situation in every family. Throughout my life, my father stayed with us only for brief periods. However, the LTTE couldn't hold Batticaloa town for long because the army retaliated by land, water and air. As a result, the LTTE retreated to Batticaloa district's border villages, separated by backwaters and dense forest. The LTTE built a strong base and ran a parallel government with infrastructure for schools, police stations, hospitals and courts.

A few years later, I was old enough to understand that something was happening in the country. The LTTE came to Batticaloa town at night and planted landmines near the army camps or the tracks where army trucks were operating during the daytime. The following days were disastrous when those landmines exploded. Not only army trucks but also civilian vehicles were blown up. Many innocent people died in such attacks as collateral damage. But even though the attacks by the LTTE affected ordinary people, the angry army rounded up our towns and villages and killed innocent people to take their revenge. But I was born in the conflict zone, so growing up there was normal for me. For kids of our age, any bombings or shootouts sounded like an action film because we were used to it, and we were not at an age to understand the consequences.

I started going to a school called Methodist Central College. My school was started in 1814 by a Methodist missionary, and it is the second oldest school in Sri Lanka. However, the schools in the conflict zones were not well maintained and developed. My school didn't even have functional toilets, and we had to use open land as toilets, which was one of my real nightmares as a child. Students were the ones who were cleaning the school buildings, and trouble-making students cleaned more than others. We didn't have teachers, or very few quality teachers, nor advanced infrastructure. I had been very interested in fine arts since I was a child, but our art teacher was also the watchman of the school who never came to class to teach us.

My parents wanted us to eat well, stay safe, and survive the night because every day from 6 pm to 6 am, a curfew was put in place to prevent LTTE infiltration. The LTTE were crossing the borders by backwaters, using catamarans that wouldn't make a noise as motorized boats would. Many nights were bright because the watchtower of the army camp next to our home shot flares (battlefield illumination) during the attacks. When we heard the sounds of gunshots and shelling, the next day my friends and I would go to the spots to collect bullet cases, as a fun activity. Because of that, it was easy for militant groups to radicalize youngsters in the war zone. Most youngsters from uneducated families joined the militant groups. Once twelve of the school students decided to join the LTTE. All but two of them died while trying to cross the dense forest borders between the army and the LTTE. The other two were brought back from the LTTE by their parents and put in special juvenile homes.

Attacks and retaliation from both sides were getting worse. Once, the LTTE bombed our public market where the army was picking up their food supplies. Many army personnel and many locals died. As revenge, the army kept raiding villages, abusing women and killing men. After many years, my father came to visit us, and he was taken by the army and kept in custody for investigations. They suspected that he was with the LTTE because there was someone in the LTTE with a similar name. As usual, he couldn't stay long because of continuous harassment from the army and the LTTE. After that, my mom was taken into custody by the LTTE, and they asked her to pay a million rupees at that time; otherwise, they would lock her in a bunker.

In 2000, a ceasefire was mediated in Sri Lanka by neutral countries like Norway, and we thought the conflict would be resolved. However, both parties used the ceasefire to restock themselves with weapons and soldiers to enter the third decade of the war. The longer the war, the younger the soldiers who were recruited. The LTTE announced a new rule in our region that every Tamil family had to give a boy or a girl above ten years old for the fight. I was in a dire situation and risked becoming a child soldier at the age of fourteen. These forced recruitments by the LTTE were happening in the border villages. There was nothing we could do. At that time, my father was in Saudi Arabia, and my elder brother was in Russia. So we finally decided that we would leave everything behind and flee to India. My mom, my sister, two of my cousins and I packed everything we could take for our new uncertain life and escaped Sri Lanka to India in 2001.

When we arrived at Chennai Airport in India, I didn't know that my life in this new place would be more complicated than my life in the conflict zone in Sri Lanka. First, we all went to Chidambaram – the same place where my Uncle Jeyan was sent in 1985 to be hosted by my mom's aunty. In the rush to flee from Sri Lanka, my parents hadn't planned the emigration properly. We ended up in India with a short-term tourist visa, which was expiring. Additionally, they didn't think about how we kids were going to go to school, or whether our educational certificates would be accepted in India. We started looking for houses for rent. Even though we lived in a conflict zone in Sri Lanka, we had a good clean home. In Chidambaram, all the rental houses we found were as small as pigeon houses and also not very clean. Additionally, people there didn't want to rent homes to Sri Lankan Tamils. After struggling in the new place for two months, a family friend helped us move out of Chidambaram to Chennai.

Challenges in Chennai started piling up. We moved to nine different houses in the first year because the house owners didn't want to give us a place. Some gave us a short period and threw us out because we were Sri Lankan Tamils. I still remember that one house owner asked us to leave, and she gave a reason that makes me laugh. She said that we – Sri Lankan Tamils – were paying monthly rentals. We would write a letter about it to the leader of the LTTE, and he would send a group of LTTE fighters to Chennai from Sri Lanka across the ocean to kidnap her. She was scared, so we had to leave her house. After that, many house owners denied us housing, calling us terrorists – referring to the Indian prime minister's assassination – when I was only 15 years old.

At that time, I didn't have a personal computer. So I decided to improve my technical and digital skills by myself, learning at an internet cafe. Most kids my age were going to the internet cafes to play computer games, but I was learning how to make one. This is how I started my first engineering service business, at the age of 15, from the skills that I taught myself. I wouldn't have done that if I was a normal kid with a typical family, going to school. When opportunities were denied, I created my own opportunities.

I soon learned that the only way to survive in India was to become Indian. I knew that I couldn't fake any papers, but I could fake my accent and story. There is a word that is used in northern India for non-conventional ways, frugal innovation, and hacks: "Jugaad". We found out that if I could get any government certificate of an examination, then it would act as a foundation for other papers. So all I needed was a paper that proved my existence in India without revealing my identity. The jugaad that I found out was that if I could apply for a public state-level exam – usually taken in tenth grade in India – as a home-schooled student, they wouldn't ask me where I had studied before. So I found a tutorial centre in Chennai where troubled kids, who were expelled from their schools, studied for public exams. All you needed to join that tutorial college was to pay the fees. I cleared my tenth-grade exam, after only three months of preparation. With that certificate, I officially entered the Indian school system.

But the systemic oppression in India was impacting every step of my life. I couldn't even open a bank account because we were all treated as ghosts in the system. Even when I finished my twelfth-grade school exam with 94.75 per cent, I was not given university admission, and I had to find an Indian jugaad again even to enrol in a substandard university. The four years of my life at university were full of different challenges. My mental health and my skills were deteriorating, and the depression which I had been suffering started getting suicidal. Neither of my parents was ready to listen, because people in our society don't acknowledge psychological issues or mental health. After completing my university studies, I was not allowed to stay in a job because I was a Sri Lankan Tamil refugee. So I wandered across that vast country with suicidal depression and without a purpose. I couldn't leave India, and I couldn't live in India.

In the meantime, the army had surrounded the last stronghold of the LTTE. The bloody war ended on 18 May 2009. An estimated 70,000 had been killed. After countless struggles, I finally got my clearance to leave the country in 2010 and departed from the same Chennai airport where I had arrived as a child refugee. After almost ten years of exile in India, I returned to Sri Lanka. Twenty-four years of my life had gone by, through suppression and oppression. I had no idea what I was going to do in Sri Lanka. However, I felt that I was liberated from my life in India, and I didn't have to live any more as a ghost in the system.

When I went back to Sri Lanka, the country looked so different from my childhood memories. For the first time in a decade, I was meeting many of my relatives. When I was in India, I often had dreams of walking the streets of Sri Lanka again, where I grew up, and now I could do that in reality. Still, I had no guidance on what I could do in my life, so I went to Saudi Arabia with my parents. However, I learned that a friend of mine had gone to Europe on a scholarship programme, and I applied for the same programme. I got a letter from the scholarship consortium to let me know that I had been selected, with €48,000 of financial aid. It would be an opportunity to study and research at four institutions in Germany, the UK, Italy, and Japan. Only nine students from thousands of applications had been selected for this scholarship, and I was second on the list. So I packed my luggage with the few things that had defined my home while I was running from country to country and city to city in my first 24 years of life. After all these struggles, I took a flight to Berlin in 2011, this time with a lower expectation of my new beginning.

However, Berlin has become the home that accepts me. It has helped me overcome my depression, uplifted me and empowered me. Since then, I have co-founded nine organizations, worked for eight tech start-ups, researched at four research institutions, become affiliated with 23 organizations, trained 300+ young innovators, mentored 150+ deep tech start-ups, and co-created several communities for start-ups, sustainability, education and art in Asia, Europe & Africa.

But while achieving those things, I was thinking every moment about how I would take my knowledge and experience back to underserved communities in war-affected Sri Lanka. For several years, I was waiting for the right co-founder to make my idea a reality. I met Kishoth in 2015 when a common friend introduced him to me, and told me about his initiative, Sagacious Youth Lead Consortium (SYLC). At the age of 19, he had built a community to promote youth participation for community development across all the diverse ethnic and religious divides in Sri Lanka. His organization was strengthening youth partnerships in marginalized and vulnerable communities in areas that had been affected by the war. They were promoting socio-economic empowerment, societal change and equal rights for women and girls. They were creating awareness of the environment. They were building peace and reconciliation to heal the past and build the future through programmes promoting social integration and giving communities a greater voice.

In 2017 we sat together to discuss how we could empower communities in the war-affected regions of Sri Lanka in an unconventional way. Batticaloa is one of the poorest districts in Sri Lanka, and it is also underdeveloped, with no infrastructure for innovation or advanced education. We brainstormed how we could develop such an initiative. At that time, I had no idea how to achieve this, but I believed that it would definitely create an impact beyond what we could imagine. I found out that three decades of civil war in Sri Lanka had caused a massive impact on socio-economic and environmental ecosystems. Sri Lanka had become one of the least innovative countries in Asia. Sri Lanka also had a negative trade balance of nine-billion US$. Hundreds of thousands of internally displaced people were facing a massive humanitarian crisis. Ethnic tensions were on the rise. Sri Lanka had been losing more than 400 elephants a year due to human-elephant conflicts. I was sure that I would not find a better co-founder than Kishoth to tackle these challenges.

More than 1,200 NGOs were working in Sri Lanka. International Aid provided significant support, but imported solutions couldn't solve fundamental local problems sustainably. So we set out to empower locals to solve these complex local challenges. Along with that motivation, my craving to support those who went through the same life experiences as mine propelled me to co-found DreamSpace Academy. DreamSpace Academy is a non-profit social enterprise that aims to tackle socio-economic and environmental challenges through challenge-based learning, grassroots innovation and impact venture building. Our mission is to achieve sustainable development goals in Sri Lanka by empowering underserved communities, protecting environmental ecosystems, facilitating peacebuilding and fostering sustainable start-ups.

Our personalized empowerment – also known as DreamSpace Lifecycle – consists of five stages. The first stage is known as "Candidate Discovery", which starts with discovering motivated candidates from underserved communities. The second stage is known as "Maker Education", where we provide these candidates with interdisciplinary challenge-based learning in topics from storytelling to biotechnology. The third stage is known as "Grassroots Innovation", where we assist them in developing grassroots innovations for local challenges that they have experienced first-hand. The fourth stage is known as "Domain Expertise", where we develop their knowledge of their chosen area by partnering them with international subject-matter experts to work with them closely. Finally, the fifth stage is known as "Venture Building", where we build their sustainable start-ups to address socio-economic and environmental challenges. The following sections explain how we co-created this model from our real-life experiences and how this model is applied in reality.

As a child, I was highly interested in digital technology, and I looked for places where I could learn geeky things. When I became a child refugee in Chennai, India, I did not go to school initially because our papers were not accepted. So, as I mentioned, I started my first engineering service business at the age of 15 from the skills that I had taught myself. Since then, I have learned many disciplines. In Germany, I worked with various organizations in healthcare, biotechnology, advanced materials, mobility, agriculture, aerospace, energy, the automotive industry and education. I realized that to solve any real-world problems, a person or team should have interdisciplinary knowledge and skills. I didn't want trainees at DreamSpace Academy to be limited to a specific skill. I wanted to give them access to the perspective of interdisciplinarity to solve complex socio-economic and environmental challenges better. This became the second stage of our DreamSpace Lifecycle known as "Maker Education".

In April 2019, we set up our Electronics Lab, Software Lab, Mechanics Lab, Business Lab and Art Lab. I trained the trainers in designing, developing and fabricating electronic circuits, software applications, mechanical parts, etc. International experts trained the team in design thinking, business modelling, financial modelling and pitching. Local experts trained the trainees in instrumental music, photography, graphic design, spoken language, and many other disciplines. At the same time, Kishoth was engaging our dedicated team to work in peacebuilding and reconciliation, rural development, youth and women's empowerment, well-being advocacy and community-building projects, which international aid organizations supported. So we started seeing the big picture of our vision and mission. There is no other non-profit organization in Sri Lanka with the capacity and operations of DreamSpace Academy.

As we were planning the following steps, we faced the biggest challenge in Sri Lanka since the war had ended. ISIS (Islamic State in Iraq and Syria) attacked several churches and luxury hotels in 2019. This incident is known as the Easter Bombings. 267 people were killed, including 45 foreign nationals, and more than 500 were injured. One of the churches that was attacked is in Batticaloa. The country went back to a state of national emergency where armies were deployed everywhere, armed sentry posts were built, minority communities – mainly Muslim communities – were raided heavily, curfews locked people down, and fear and hate were spreading among the communities. People – who had tasted ten years of a bit of freedom and harmony since the war ended – started living in the same conditions as the wartime. We deployed our crisis response team to the places where help was needed. We sent our peacebuilding, reconciliation and well-being advocacy team to create audio-visual content to mitigate hate speech and fake news on social media. We did what we could do, but we were also impacted during this time. All our other operations were stopped. All those international experts who wanted to join us had to change their minds.

Over the years, DreamSpace Academy has produced a large number of success stories. Jayanthan is dedicated to solving plastic pollution issues in Batticaloa. He was a Duke of Edinburgh Medal winner for his work on the water and environmental advocacy. At a summit in Berlin, I met the team of the Precious Plastic community. Precious Plastic is an open-source hardware plastic recycling project from the Netherlands. It focuses on a series of machines and tools that grind, melt, and inject recycled plastic, allowing for creating new products out of recycled plastic on a small scale. This grassroots innovation was very well aligned to the challenges and interests of Jayanthan. Our version of Precious Plastic was known as "Circular Plastic", and Jayanthan reproduced the Precious Plastic machine with the support of other community members.

Initially, the team built it from cardboard. In the second iteration, they built the plastic shredder with hand-cut metal cogwheels and a pedal bike to generate power instead of electric motors. Finally, Jayanthan built a fully metal-manufactured plastic shredder. Jayanthan didn't have professional technical and vocational skills before this project, and he learned them while tackling the challenge of plastic pollution. Additionally, we trained him on business modelling, financial modelling, stakeholder management, strategy, operations and elevator pitching. Since then, at several start-up competitions, he has presented this project as "Trash for Trade" with everything from machine building and trash collection to upcycled product manufacturing. As a result, he has received more than one-million rupees in funds, making it the first social enterprise spun off from DreamSpace Academy. With those funds, he helped us build a better infrastructure for the Mechanics Lab with a welding machine, CNC machine, drill press, mitre saw, grinding machine and several power tools. Jayanthan became a role model to many fellow youngsters, and we understood that we had co-created a true change-maker.

Another DreamSpace candidate was Shanjeevan, the younger brother of Jayanthan. When we discovered him, he was just 18 and had just graduated from school. I learned that in Sri Lanka, there is often more than a one and half year gap between schooling and university because the system is slow. Additionally, the majority of universities are public, and there are not enough places for everyone. This gap impacts many talented and motivated students from underserved communities because they are not appropriately guided during this time. Some go to temporary jobs in the Middle East, and they never return to higher education because of their responsibility to earn for their families. Some become alcoholics or drift into crime. We knew that if we chose someone who hadn't finished schooling yet or was already attending university, then our model would interrupt their studies, which no parents would allow. However, with

Shanjeevan's case, we learned that this gap between school and university is ideal for bringing candidates into the DreamSpace Lifecycle.

In his school days, Shanjeevan was an active member of the Scout Association, promoting environmental protection. He and his friend had walked 435 kilometres from the north to the south tip of Sri Lanka through the forests to promote national peace. He was the first Sri Lankan Tamil teenager to climb Mount Elbrus – the highest peak of Eurasia. His motivation to tackle social and environmental challenges helped us define the acceptance criteria for our first stage of DreamSpace Lifecycle, "Candidate Discovery".

When I met him for the first time, he didn't have a clear picture of what he wanted to do professionally in life, and he didn't know his true purpose. At the same time, he was considered a rebellious kid at his home. His case taught us another important lesson: Before we set out to empower any youngster, we need to empower their parents. Parents are the decision-makers even for adults in a country like Sri Lanka. They decide everything from what their children study to whom they marry. Children are also often stuck with their parents' norms of life and societal taboos. Most parents believe that one can be successful only if they have a degree in Medicine, Engineering or Law. All other degrees are considered failures. So it was a difficult challenge to convince Shanjeevan's parents to allow him to come into DreamSpace. They wanted him to become a doctor or lawyer. However, when I spoke to him for the first time, it was evident that he had no interest in medicine or law. Finally, they agreed to let him work with us for 12 months before admission to a reputable public university.

Within our Lifecycle, we identified that Shanjeevan's domain of interest was water. Batticaloa has an area of 2,854 km², and 244 km² of that are flat year-round warm-water shallow-lagoons, thus making it a breeding ground for a diverse range of plants and animals. However, there has been a steep decline in biodiversity. The backwaters have been affected by agricultural runoffs of nitrate and phosphate. The ocean species, especially native species like manta rays, sharks, seahorses and seagrass, have been affected by illegal fishing vessels. Sri Lanka claims an Exclusive Economic Zone (EEZ) extending 200 nautical miles – covering approximately 6.7 times Sri Lanka's land area – that provides massive economic value to this small nation. Shanjeevan did his due diligence on this challenge with the support of local experts. He comes from the coastal region of Batticaloa, and he clearly saw the impact of marine biodiversity degradation on his society. Therefore, he came back with an affirmation that protecting the blue ecosystems was his true purpose.

To keep our water ecosystem safe, secure, clean and sustainable, we need to measure multi-parameter underwater data in real-time so that environmental authorities and conservation organizations can make informed decisions. Several solutions are available, such as Autonomous Underwater Vehicles (AUV), which gather real-time oceanographic data for an extended duration and distance, with minimal human effort. However, such commercial solutions could cost around €200,000, and extraordinary expertise and high costs are involved in maintaining and repairing such systems. Thus such solutions are not suitable for Sri Lanka. Nevertheless, there has been a breakthrough with low-cost autonomous underwater vehicles, and as this capability has matured, a wide range of hobby and commercial applications have been developed.

Underwater gliders use a buoyancy engine to change their mass, allowing them to ascend and descend through the water. With energy only being used to power the engine intermittently, gliders can typically run for weeks or months without a recharge, making them ideal for environmental monitoring. As underwater gliders travel slowly through the water, they disturb the surrounding water very little, allowing for accurate and reliable data recording. Therefore, Shanjeevan decided to build this as his grassroots innovation. Before Shanjeevan started working with us, he didn't have any technical expertise in design, electronics, mechanics, software, digital fabrication or even oceanology. With this most pressing challenge to protect our blue ecosystems, he earned those interdisciplinary skills in an impactful way using our challenge-based learning methodology.

In a short period, he developed those complex engineering skills. As a result, he built the first functional underwater glider in Sri Lanka that cost around €2,000, a hundred times cheaper than the imported ones and an open innovation, able to be maintained, repaired and upgraded by anyone. Such a solution would not only be useful for Sri Lanka but also useful for many other countries in the Global South. Shanjeevan's work has been featured in international and national media and even mentioned in the parliament of Sri Lanka. His dedication to this local innovation proved that the victims of any challenges are better candidates to solve them, because those challenges are an everyday reality for them.

In the fourth stage, "Domain Expertise", we amplify the domain-specific knowledge of our candidates by partnering them with international experts and organizations. So we presented Shanjeevan's story to Oceanic Platform of the Canary Islands (PLOCAN), a singular scientific and technological infrastructure established by the European Union. PLOCAN's research centre is located in the Atlantic Ocean and conducts deep-sea explorations with heavily equipped underwater infrastructure. PLOCAN accepted Shanjeevan's application and requested him to come to Gran Canaria, the Canary Islands, to train him in their Glider School programme. He also presented the project to Dr Asha De Vos. Her work to protect the blue whales within the northern Indian Ocean is phenomenal. However, her team has to collect multi-parameter underwater data. When we identified that Shanjeevan's locally-made underwater glider solution could be of great value and support for researchers in Sri Lanka like Asha, we knew that Shanjeevan was perfectly ready to build his own organization – either for-profit or non-profit – to continue his ocean tech and advocacy work with a dedicated team. With that experience, we perfected our last stage of the DreamSpace Lifecycle known as "Venture Building".

After working with us for 18+ months, Shanjeevan reached the end of our DreamSpace Lifecycle to graduate as a change-maker. He built his organization, "OceanBiome", where 25+ young oceanologists and advocates work with him to tackle the most pressing challenges of marine ecosystems by co-creating open innovations and teaching ocean literacy. Sri Lanka is a country known for tea and tourism where there are not many industries and innovations in advanced science and deep technology domains. When someone studies oceanology, therefore, the only respectable job that they could get in the country would be a clerical job in a bank. So with our model, we are not only building a change-maker but also an industry that can mature in ten to twenty years. Thus our youngsters won't have to go abroad for opportunities or to become low-cost manual workers or asylum seekers. This is the true meaning of sustainable socio-economic and environmental development for us.

There are also other very promising DreamSpace candidates. Abinaya was discovered in early 2020 when her chemistry teacher presented her. Abinaya came from a border forest village in Batticaloa with limited access to education and advanced infrastructure. However, with her motivation to solve water challenges, she developed a simple biofilter made from the seed of the java plum – a purple-coloured fruit native to the Indian subcontinent and Southeast Asia – to filter cadmium pollution in the water. In short, she co-created an organic nanotechnology solution while being in a region of the world where people don't even know about nanotechnology or the presence of cadmium in the water due to metal pipes or agricultural runoffs. When we discovered her, she was just sixteen years old, and we coached her on how to write a scientific paper and presented her to Stockholm International Water Institute

(SIWI). As a result, she won the Stockholm Junior Water Prize in 2020 among applications from 40 countries in the Global South.

Since we constantly seek collaboration with international aid organizations, we approached the Skills for Inclusive Growth (S4IG) initiative from Australian Aid with the aim of training twenty visual content makers around ecotourism topics. Skill development in ecotourism is one of the mandates of Australian Aid. Unlike most NGOs and social enterprises, we were willing to integrate our model into this programme, and our proposal was accepted. Funds allocated for this project helped us to survive the COVID-19 pandemic. Twenty-seven youngsters from underserved communities around Sri Lanka were incubated for eight months to be trained in storytelling, camera handling, digital portfolio creation, business and financial modelling, and digital marketing. We didn't just train them with skills but also empowered them to build a business out of it, so they didn't have to look for jobs elsewhere. In this way, we were not just providing a livelihood to underserved communities; instead, we co-created their intellectual livelihood. That is why our motto is "Co-creating dreams".

Many of those trainees built studios, and among them, Basith's story is very inspiring. He comes from an underserved Muslim community where most people are traders, and higher education is not accessible to many. His father is a speechless person, and because of that, he was not given any respectable job. Basith was educated thanks to funds from a charity based in the UK. He didn't have any exposure to advanced studies or skills. With his learnings from the S4IG programme, Basith created his own studio for photography, videography, graphic design and digital marketing. During the pandemic time, he reached out to small shop owners in his region, took photos and videos, created online social media pages for them, set up door delivery services and carried out performance marketing campaigns. He helped around ten local shop owners through the economic crisis of the pandemic.

Another unconventional team member is Cris, because he is the first Sinhalese person to move to Batticaloa to work with us. He was trained in biotechnology in Colombo and worked as a research assistant at the University of Peradeniya. He quit his academic career to join our mission to build the first community bio lab in Sri Lanka. With his arrival into our team, we are changing the narrative that people have to migrate to major cities for opportunities, because we create opportunities in sectors that don't even exist in the capital city. This is true peacebuilding for us, because we are uniting all religious and ethnic groups of Sri Lanka with a passion for education, innovation and entrepreneurship. Not only Sri Lankans but also international change-makers are joining our team. One of them is Cosmo, who moved to Batticaloa in 2021 from the Netherlands.

In summary, the impact and achievements of DreamSpace in the last few years are enormous. We empowered 520+ underserved youngsters from underserved communities. We established eight community labs. We co-created nine grassroots innovations. We spun off eight social enterprises and initiatives. We received 23 medals from The Duke of Edinburgh's Award. We won the Falling Walls

Award 2019, Peace Direct Award 2019, Global Bio Fellowship 2020 and nine more awards. We were featured by BBC, Die Zeit, Les Echos and fifteen more international media.

Throughout my life, I often thought, "I don't have any reason to live in this world." I often asked myself, "If I'm still alive after surviving such threatening incidents, what is my life's purpose?" Millions of people like us from the Global South are dying yearly because of preventable diseases like malaria, dengue and zika. We still don't have a reliable solution for that. But at the same time, within a year of the coronavirus affecting the Global North, solutions began to emerge everywhere because it is also the problem of developed nations. So we are the ones who should be tackling our own fundamental challenges. I think I have found my true purpose: to dedicate my life to empowering children and youngsters from underserved communities anywhere in the world to tackle their challenges and co-create their dreams. My journey to impact will continue.

Thanks to my friends and well-wishers: Ganapathy, Velmohan, Sathish, Mythili, Anand, Joseph, Navaneethan, Soundararajan, Mohit, Deepti, Sneha, Bhargav and many more for helping me out to survive in India. Thanks to my wife, Natasha; my friends in Berlin: Mladen, Carlos, Ana, Ivana, Maite, Darina, Ahmad, Federico and many more; my parents, Panch and Chandra; my brother, Hari; my sister, Tharaneya, and uncle Jeyan for being part of my success story. DreamSpace wouldn't have been possible without my core team members: Kishoth, Jeyanthan, Shanjeevan, Basith, Jerushan, Gunarakulan, Abilajini, Abitharani, Rishanthini, Faahim, Kamini, Anna,

Cris, Nafha, Thanushkar, Pavithran, Azath, Cosmo and many more.

Kadana's Story

Akinyi Awora (Kenya)

Today I ran six kilometres. It's not a newsworthy distance, but I ran it, I liked it, and now you are reading about it. My record so far is 13 kilometres (I do not know what that is in miles). I am Kenyan – not that it has anything to do with my running, I just thought it would create more context. Anyway, the thing about my run today was it was inspiring – and no, I did not have any spiritual awakening, I just had a laugh while at it. I don't get to laugh a lot, haven't in a while, but today I did.

About three kilometres into my run, the trail starts going uphill. Today I was not just going uphill but I had about two extra kilograms of mud on my shoes. I am not exaggerating; I am just going by what it felt like. This part of the trail is usually unforgiving, but the extra weight made it almost impossible.

So I am trudging uphill trying to get the mud off my shoes and run at the same time, because slowing down at this section will take you out. In front of me, there is this little girl walking to school and she starts walking fast, testing whether I am running as slow as it seems. I have longer strides so I catch up to her eventually, and stop to get the mud off my shoes, but what I really want is to give her a head start. So now I am running again and I catch up to her – only this time, she is running as well. Now we are having our own enactment of the Tokyo Olympics. Further up the hill, another young girl in gumboots is watching what I imagine was something between awkward and strange. A grown woman and a little girl running, half panting, half giggling. Anyway, as we get closer, it turns out the two little girls know each other; I hear the one that was with me calling out to the other. Now the three of us are running, the girls trying to run faster and me torn between winning against two little girls and losing to two little girls. Either way, I lose. We get to a particularly steep section of the hill, and they are wiped out. Therefore, now I am coaching and running, because I cannot leave my motivation behind. We get to the top, the trail straightens out, and I run off towards the rest of my path and they wave at me as they take the detour to school.

Here is the thing: I am in rural western Kenya, and those little girls have never seen a grown woman run. It's not a lot, but today they learned something new about being a woman. We can run, and we can run uphill with two kilograms of mud on our shoes.

The thing about those girls was that they reminded me of a time when living was a true embodiment of Winnie the Pooh's philosophies. When happiness was unconditional, and living was not based on how many cautionary tales we were trying to duck, but on what wonders you conjured in your imagination. When I was brave without thinking. A time when I laughed.

My only memory from this time was when I woke up one morning and the other kids were gone. I remember going to get my usual cup of milk from my Dana (grandma) and no one was there. The milk was where it usually was: On the kitchen floor, in a cup covered by a large sufuria (metal pot) so the cat could not get to it. Milk was usually the first breakfast – I had at least one meal and two snacks before lunch, since I was my Dana's favourite. I just thought everyone had gone off to the farm, so I had my milk, and went off playing. I never had any problem being in my own company. I had enough friends to keep me company – well, only I could see them, but hey, we were just fine.

Anyway, it was soon lunchtime and everyone was

coming in, from farms, schools or wherever it was that people went, I did not know. One of my cousins, (who I later learned was actually my aunty – polygamous family dynamics are weird) and the only person in my age group then, came in. She had on new clothes and new shoes, but that was not what caught my attention. She kept on singing this rhyme and I asked her to teach me. She refused. Later that evening, she and some of the older kids sang rhymes running around the compound, playing new games I did not understand. I don't know whether it's a natural trait or if it's something I learned somewhere, but I do not like not knowing things. To this date, I seek out knowledge, compulsively. It's a disease. Anyway, my three-year-old self hatched a plan. I simply would go to where they went, and then I would learn the rhymes and would show them. I know how it sounds: I was three, gimme a break.

So I picked out my favourite shorts and shoes and went to bed in them. I did not sleep much. The next day, I waited till my cousin was up and ready to go and sneaked up behind them all the way to the new school. I just walked in and sat down. The teacher never noticed anything until around half past noon when my Dana came in to pull my cousin out of class to find out whether she had seen me and saw me there instead. On the way home, she asked me whether I liked it there. I said all we did was sing, and that had gotten boring pretty fast. She laughed, we got home and she gave me my milk. I still went back the next day, boring or not. The race had begun and I was not getting left behind. This is my earliest memory of being brave.

About six months later, my mom came and got me

and we moved to a place in central Kenya called Ruiru. This is where I learned I was a girl. I know you are wondering, 'But she was a girl the entire time – how could she not know?' Before Ruiru it never mattered. I wore whatever pleased me (I preferred shorts), and did whatever I wanted, within safe and reasonable bounds. There was this neighbour in Ruiru that was like an uncle. In fact, all I know of his name was Uncle. I used to get candy and stuff from Uncle; my mama knew him from the church choir, so she was comfortable with me being around him. I don't remember exactly when but Uncle's brother came visiting, and I remember going to Uncle's house to pick at the box of army biscuits he would leave by the table for me and found a stranger. I was around six at this time and knew not to talk to strangers, so I ran back to our house to wait until Uncle came back.

Later on in the evening, Uncle comes knocking at our door and asks my ma why I did not come for my biscuits that day. So he tells my ma about the visiting brother and tells me, 'Huyo ni Uncle Mdogo' (That is your small uncle). So the next day I go for my box as always and find Uncle Mdogo, but my box of biscuits is not where I used to get it from. I ask him where it is and he says I did not greet him, and it's bad manners, so I do not get my biscuits until I apologize. I say I am sorry. But he just stands there holding my box of biscuits hostage. What I remember the most is his smile. Not smirk, smile. It was not threatening, not at all. If anything, it was reassuring. I knew I was going to get the box in the end, so I played along.

He looks at me and asks whether I want to show

him I am sorry. I agree and, out of the blue, Uncle Mdogo drops his pants. I am six years old, so I am giggling because I have never seen a grown man naked. Then he says that if I touch the thing, he is going to let me have my biscuits.

The rest of the story goes how these stories usually go. About a month later, Uncle Mdogo disappeared and we moved to Ruaraka. This was my introduction to power dynamics. My shoes had started collecting mud.

I don't remember much from Ruaraka. My life revolved around school work and advanced classes. My friends lived mostly in books. I don't know how or when, but somewhere in between I stopped laughing. I was always in trouble. I don't even remember why, but I know it had something to do with never really doing as I was told, or asking too many questions. Eventually I got shipped to boarding school. Well, it turns out that a little bit of truancy makes you a pseudo-celebrity. I got in trouble for reading novels during lessons and for commenting on teachers' hairstyles or sometimes just for being. I absolutely abhorred the idea of someone else having a veto on who I was and how I was to be. I did not know it yet, but I had been angry for a very long time. When my dad died, and we got kicked out of our house, somehow the volcano erupted.

I was every bit of psychological disorder on the spectrum – again, not exaggerating, just calling it as I saw it. I don't even know how I got involved, but I remember a girl at the school being bullied because of rumours that she was gay. I didn't even know what that meant at the time but what the girls were doing to her did not sit right with me. I remember calling some girls off, and offering to speak at assembly, where I called out an entire school and teachers for being shitty human beings. I don't even know how but the story ended up with me being suspended because I refused to take the punishment, when I did nothing wrong.

This was the beginning of me channelling whatever madness I had going on inside me into something constructive. It is how, on campus, I advocated for and successfully got the university administration to make new policies that allowed for student representation. I relied solely on student loans and got by. I am the type of person that is curious about people. So I talk to my motorbike rider, or get to know more about the school cook. You see, I had learned a very important lesson in school. I never really had pocket money and relied solely on school meals but the cooks in the kitchen sneaked me food from the deputy principal's diet. On campus, when the loans were late and I could not pay for housing in time, the support staff that did the booking always got me a room until the money came in. Until this day, I make security guards and cleaning people my friends because they might not be management, but the very people we deem invisible hold these places together.

In my third year on campus, I got pregnant. I had always had issues with extreme malaria before, but what I did not know was how fatal it can be for a pregnant woman. I remember being hospitalized five times during the entire course of the pregnancy and all of those times, I had severe malaria. The last time ended up killing the baby just one week before she was due. I did not know she was dead until when I was admitted to the hospital for delivery. I don't remember most of what happened. What my mother told me was that my baby died, and I almost did. I haemorrhaged and it took an act of God and three pints of blood to keep me alive.

I was an unmarried woman who had lost a child. Apparently in Luo tradition that makes you unclean. This meant isolation. You do not leave a grieving woman alone. I don't remember how long it was, but I know I saw the devil's face in those weeks I was in that tiny room away from everyone else. Eventually my mother had to travel to Nairobi for something, so I sneaked back home. All I wanted was to be with family. She came back and in the middle of the night kicked me out. I cannot explain what this does to an already broken spirit.

I was working as an online writer then, so I had money for transport to go back to school. However, I did not have any other money, so I made an agreement with the person I was writing for to give me an advance of 3,000 Kenyan shillings (KES) to settle the hostel fees. When I got to campus, I could not reach him, so I stayed at my friends' house. Friends in plural – it was a single room that housed four men. The next day I started getting sick. I had a severe headache and could not stand upright without veering. By this time, the dispensary already knew I was from western Kenya, so I always had a test for malaria. I ended up being hospitalized again. On the day I got discharged, I realized I was homeless. I was anaemic, on anti-malarial drugs and I had not eaten for three days. My mother had flat-out refused to send me money, my uncle whom I had been living with had to call her and she finally sent me money which I told her I would pay back as soon as my loan got disbursed. For whatever reason the money never got disbursed that semester. I somehow got through. I remember using other students' exam cards or pretending to have forgotten mine just to get through exams. I could never afford the graduation fees so my degree certificate is still at the university.

A kind woman agreed to buy most of my things, which is how I funded my transport home after the last exam. I started giving literacy classes for free to a friend of mine that had left school due to the lack of fees. Eventually I discovered Lakehub. Lakehub is described as 'a technology, creative and social innovation hub' and what it meant for me was having a community of young people unafraid to take chances, which changed my view of the world. It was while at Lakehub that with 300 KSE, my two friends and a camera, we walked around Obunga slums in Kisumu collecting stories of resilience. I knew very little about development programmes, but I knew enough to know that the world was being fed a single story and that it was not the whole story.

Later on that year, I walked into my friend's office (she was an intern at the county government), to find her applying for what she called the Mandela Washington Fellowship. I had no idea what it was, but the three-year-old in me that does not get left behind got into action. I remember the day I got the call that I had been shortlisted. The morning before I had asked my cousin for twenty shillings that I would give back in the evening. It was a particularly hot day in Kisumu and I was feeling a little bit unwell, so I could not walk to the hub. I was relying on my friend being there. She was how I was going to pay the 20 bob back, but she did not come to the hub that day. I remember my aunt laughing as my cousin cursed me out for pretending to be better than everyone else when I could not even afford 20 shillings. I learned early on in life that you never let people see you cry, and although my tears are usually scarce, on that day I cried.

The next day, around 11 am, I got a strange call from a lady who wanted to know whether I was Eulalia. I did not know who she was and nobody I know ever calls me by my first name. I remember her chiding me for not having phone etiquette, but I did not care after she told me I was shortlisted and that they needed me in Nairobi the next day. Then she asked me whether I wanted to go by bus or by air. I had only ever seen aeroplanes in movies – I didn't even get the primary school airport tour – so of course I went for the air option. Anyway, the next day I was on a flight to Nairobi.

I have always been able to adapt, I will change colours or do whatever it takes to survive. Nothing prepared me for the Magna Suites and Hotels. I have eaten food out of someone else's trash can but it took a fancy hotel, people that spoke English plus other languages and fancy clothes to shake me. I just sat there quiet, while everyone else networked. I caught glimpses of CVs that had PhDs. I was just in a dress and Bata rubber shoes, and I did not even have a wallet. I carried my identification card in my hand and nobody had told me that people brought CVs to interviews let alone that people owned CVs. Anyway, I went in for the interview. I may not have had anything fancy about me, but what I had was the story of a girl who wanted to fight for a better education system, for better development processes. I knew nothing about policy, I just knew that the ones we had did not work, and I promised that panel that all I needed was one person who believed it could be done. They gave me the chance: a month later I was on my way to Washington DC.

DC was the beginning of learning. It was the first time I saw where I was from and who I was from a different perspective. I got the chance to ask questions to those of whom I had always wanted to ask questions. I had no media or diplomacy training; I often fell in trouble. The thing is, I am very comfortable being uncomfortable. I came back in 2017 and started actively organizing young people to ask the questions I had learned to ask. To realize that it was our job to get things done because there is no Superman. I started a legacy programme in 2017, working with out of school youth. My goal was simple, I was going to build a platform that gave everyone a chance, just like I got one.

In the beginning I had no idea how to run any programme, I simply organized classes and developed a curriculum that included employability and entrepreneurship skills. I knew nothing about the legal processes involved. And I had no source of reference aside from what I heard from people and what I could find on the internet. So I got a consultant, who never delivered. Eight months in, I had started gaining a little bit of traction, and that came with unwanted attention. I was running out of funding and had to choose between running the programme and paying school fees for my younger sister. I had to find a way to make money.

A month later, at a networking event organized by the Segal Family Foundation, I talked to a consultant about the idea of bringing together the team of young people that had been volunteering for our events under the banner of a registered company. The point was to be paid for what we were good at. Me for my ideas and ability to imagine systems out of nothing and the rest for an assortment of capabilities. We were young people with bold ideas but zero experience running a business. Besides, I had left campus, got into a fellowship, completed that and gone straight into being a parent. Start-ups work if the founders involved have some level of safety net. I was running a start-up with no safety net. My money went to putting my siblings through school. They are not my children, but they are my responsibility. Six months in, it all imploded. Now, I had no company and no money, but by then both my siblings had cleared high school. I left and joined a microfinance organization where I ran a business-training programme for women. I had gone into a partnership, but it turned out I was to be no more than the poster girl and would not have any real influence. I had been the very woman the organization was claiming to help and I was not going to walk my talk. So again I left. Then the pandemic hit.

The year 2020 was in every way me running up the steepest part of the hill with mud on my shoes. I was tired. So I built a tandoor, and tilled the farm. I grew rosemary and lemon grass. I woke up one morning and ran for ten minutes to clear my head. I kept running every day. By the time I had built myself up to running for 30 minutes, I had worked through the first half of my plan for KUZA, a system change initiative that would work with women and drive new opportunities for rural economic growth. KUZA had a simple mission, in my mind, to provide sustainable business development and financing services to female entrepreneurs in rural and peri-urban areas in Kenya. Thirty minutes does not seem like a lot, but it is when you are obese. When I was able to run three kilometres, I asked one of my cousins to introduce me to some women and youth groups he was involved with. I walked five kilometres to the place where they used to meet. They were the representatives of eleven women's, self-help and youth groups in Karemo division, and I pitched the idea of KUZA. They asked if I could do individual group visits and I said yes. I had zero resources, but I had a plan. I walked back home and adjusted KUZA based on the information I had got from the groups. At this point I knew that for KUZA to work, we needed a digital platform. My phone had been faulty for a while but for some reason I got it to work that day. I sent please-call-me texts to all the people I thought could help. Only one of them replied. I pitched what I wanted to do and he asked me to send a write-up. When I told him I had no way to, he sent me phone credit and for the first time in a year, I was back online. The second I got back online, I knew it was only a matter of time. About a week later, a friend reached out. He had been building this platform and he did not have the slightest idea or resources to get it off the ground. So I told him I also needed a digital platform but could not afford a developer. It was at this point that KUZA found a home. Kadana was born out of sheer serendipity.

Kadana Foundation, our organization, has the mission to create smart, resilient, and economically efficient communities in Kenya and East Africa. Through human-centred design, we aim to harness the innovations of the fourth industrial revolution – the latest evolving technology – to solve social challenges in health, education and economic empowerment, eventually creating smart, resilient, and sustainable communities. Kadana Foundation was now able to launch, with KUZA as one of its flagship projects.

About two weeks later, my first round of group visits were due. I did not know how it was going to happen, but I woke up and started walking in the direction of the first group I was to visit. I walked for a bit to cut on the transport costs until I got to the centre where we had met the groups for the first time. I had zero shillings, no phone credit, a phone that was likely to die anytime and no idea where I was going. I took a motorbike and gave the guy a name; he said he knew where that was so we left. Turned out, he did not know where he was going so a 30-minute bike ride turned into an hour and a half. Eventually, we asked our way around until we got there. I told the chairperson of the group I was visiting that I had an issue with my phone and did not have cash on me, so he paid for the bike guy. While all this was going down, my partner was running around Kisumu on a motorbike to pawn his TV. We got 7,000 shillings, and did six group visits in two days.

I finally had enough information to put KUZA together. So, I texted an old friend, Sadiq, in South Africa and explained what we were doing. At this point there were two of us: Brian, my co-founder, and myself. Sadiq asked me to send a write up, and I told him I could not because I was using free WhatsApp. So he called from Richards Bay in South Africa, and asked me to pitch. I did, and he invested 60,000 KES to start with. A month later, Kadana had three partners, Brian, Sadiq and myself.

I reached out to Just People's, a group that I had met earlier on in 2019. It is an Australian charity run by two amazing ladies named Christey and Jo. I pitched the KUZA programme, which was to work with women's groups to establish social enterprises that solved gaps within their communities in education, healthcare and economic development. The KUZA programme was now refined and aimed to use digital tools to streamline rural economies in three ways. First by creating KUZA clubs which would allow rural women to share their labour and technical skills and access learning platforms. Secondly create KUZA Capital which would provide them with social investment finance, and thirdly KUZA cooperatives, which would allow groups of women to come together to serve larger markets at scale.

I told Christey and Jo that we had not received official certification yet but they agreed to raise money for our pilot KUZA project (GENO), which involved training groups of seamstresses in the production of modified baby wraps that would be used in maternity hospitals across rural western Kenya. The product was a powerless incubator wrap, used in kangaroo mother care units, where mothers use their own bodies as incubators for the preterm babies because newborn care units in rural Kenya do not have electric incubators

I had been offline for a year, so I had 12 months' backlog on email. I had gotten a WhatsApp message from a lady called Serina asking whether I had been able to register for the One Young World summit in Munich. The annual One Young World Summit convenes the brightest young talent from every country and sector, working to accelerate social impact. One Young World identifies, promotes and connects the world's most impactful young leaders to create a better world, with more responsible, more effective leadership. I had applied for the One Young World Enterprise for Peace Scholarship and had no idea I had gotten in, let alone that scholars were taking part in the academy courses. I explained this to Serina, who helped me register for the summit. A month later I saw a call for delegate speakers and did not apply initially, but when I thought the deadline had passed I saw that there was an extension and decided to apply. Eventually, I got an email letting me know I had been selected as a delegate speaker. About two minutes later, I got another email saying that I did not make it. I did not know which of those emails was right and I did not want to ask lest it was the second one. I was at the peak of the hill and slowing down would take me out. Anyway, later on I got an email confirming I had gotten in.

My One Young World speech was filmed by phone in front of our farm with cows and chickens gunning to make an appearance as well. My experience, even though virtual, was one of a kind. I met young people from all over the world on a mission to change the world. I even dare say

I made some friends. The One Young World Summit in Munich debuted the Kadana Foundation. I would not have gotten halfway through the speech were it not for Ian and Oli, who were working for One Young World, cheering me along as I wrote and filmed my speech. Sadiq and Brian, my partners, took on my workload to ensure I had the full experience.

Depending on your perspective, you read resilience, or kindness, or pain. But the point of this story is not that I pulled through. Unbelievably, my experience is generic: I work with girls and women to whom this story is familiar. The point of this story is, we can change stories like these, before the little girls stop laughing and start living one cautionary tale after the other. The point of this story is that you can be the deciding difference.

Kadana means "grandma's" or "grandma's place". When I was looking for a name for my fresh start, I wanted something that reminded me of the little girl that admitted herself to nursery school, the girl that laughed. I wanted something that reminded me of my creative confidence, and the only time I could remember was that time at grandma's place, Kadana.

So tomorrow I will still run. I cannot stop now; I have cleared the hill; maybe eventually I will get better shoes that are non-sticky and do not collect two kilograms of mud. Maybe I will have my motivation squad with me, but I know one thing for sure – I will be laughing while at it.

Voices for Thought

A conversation between our Outreach Germany Coordinator Margot Ossola, VOICE writer Maisam Abumorr and Outreach Africa Coordinator and VOICE writer Sheila Chepkoech.

Maisam

Maisam Abumorr is one of our VOICE writers. She joined VOICE in 2017 and shared her story in our last book, *A Definition of Snow*. Maisam is a political and women's rights activist from Palestine. She studied linguistics, political science and sociology. As an analyst and researcher, she works on the Middle East and North Africa (MENA) region with a particular expertise in gender, human rights and civil societies. She currently lives in London and works as a news analyst at Facebook.

Sheila

Sheila Chepkoech currently serves as the regional contact for Africa at VOICE and is in charge of our Outreach programme in Kenya. Sheila joined VOICE in 2016 at its foundation. She studied International Relations and International Development. She is an international development and higher education professional with great interest and passion in finding solutions to challenges facing young people within the society she grew up in. She currently lives in Eldoret in Kenya.

Maisam

Why did you join VOICE as a writer?

Growing up knowing I'd take a different path from that drawn for me by my circumstances, I always sought guidance in other people's journeys but found very few that I could relate to. While my journey is far from over, I'm hoping that another woman, somewhere out there, can find parts of herself in my story and that she finds comfort in the fact that she's not alone.

What made you become an activist for human rights?

I don't know. I never thought it was a choice I consciously made. I simply found myself in situations where I thought to myself, "this can't be right". And contrary to most of those around me, deep down, I believed that there must be something that could be done about it. So, my "activism" is merely me trying to navigate my understanding of my surroundings and *choosing not to accept* injustice, especially when it comes in the form of "the status quo".

What are the main social, economic, and cultural challenges in your home country?

I am a woman from a third world country currently living under occupation. That harbours multiple layers of complicated challenges. Being a woman anywhere is a constant fight. Being a woman of colour in a third world country under a brutal occupation is like finding yourself surrounded by battles from every possible direction at all times. You're fighting the limitations imposed on your gender identity within your own community and then you're fighting the continuous attempts to wipe out your national identity by the conflict. All of this while fighting on other fronts for mere daily survival, for racial justice, for equal pay, for renting rights … fighting to be heard at all.

Do you think that MENA is an appropriate label to cover the varied experiences lived in the regions?

Of course, sharing a language, a history and a broad cultural identity makes the region stand as a unit and some accurate general conclusions can be drawn from looking at MENA as one region. But stopping there is what causes inaccurate – and often harmful – generalizations. My experience as a Palestinian woman from Gaza is fundamentally different from that of a Saudi woman from Riyadh despite some similarities on the surface.

What are your thoughts on the way women in the MENA region are portrayed in Western discourses?

I find it too common that both media and academia directed at the masses (as opposed to more complicated, niche analyses) opt to oversimplify truths to facilitate consumption. That's exactly how stereotyping is such a popular method in boxing 'other' people's experiences and reducing them to general themes. This is not only inaccurate and lazy, it is outright dangerous. When, for instance, you define all women from conflict zones as victims, you deprive them of opportunities that could help them and the coming generations to override their circumstances. It's like offering a bread basket to a person dying of extreme cold. They can't do much with it.

Maisam, you currently live in the UK. How does your experience of inequality differ between where you come from (MENA) and where you reside now (Europe)? Any patterns or striking differences?

Living here added more battles to an already beaten-up soldier as additional forms of inequality and consequences of stereotyping started shaping my everyday life. There are the obvious ones like the long immigration process, re-entering the job market, adjusting to new gender-based challenges like equal pay. But there are the less obvious ones like renting, opening a bank account, dating, adjusting to unfamiliar professional and social dynamics. Back home my experiences were shaped by being a Palestinian woman in a patriarchal society under Israeli occupation. Now I'm an unnamed immigrant woman of colour.

Many experts postulate that some combination of institutionalized legal discrimination, cultural practices, lack of education and religious beliefs about women contribute to gender inequality in the MENA region and in Africa. In what ways can women's rights be advanced to ensure gender equality?

I believe that this is the root to all discrimination across the world and along its history, and now practiced on both visible and invisible levels, not only in the regions mentioned. I know this is a complicated issue and entire books have been written to attempt to answer this question. However, from my own experience, an effective starting point would be for women to support other women above anything else. There's nothing more painful than seeing women contributing to discriminating against other women. Being passive and choosing not to use your voice to combat inequality is also inexcusable. This is not to say that the responsibility falls on those discriminated against to combat injustice because we all know that's a force beyond one specific gender. This is a call to start with building internal solidarity that will give us the needed ammunition to move on to engaging in the ultimate fight.

Sheila

Sheila, why did you join VOICE?

Growing up in a developing country and later on getting into development studies, I was often taken aback with the glorification of efforts from the West in "saving" Africans. Often the narrative in development does not tell the full story of people coming from these countries who are constantly working towards making their societies better. I joined VOICE because it is a platform that gives the other side of the story. Instead of projecting people from countries such as mine as victims, it tells their stories of resilience, agency and the efforts they put in every day to make their world a better place. VOICE empowers people in developing countries by giving them a platform to showcase their resilience and agency in solving challenges they face through sharing their stories. This side of the story is not so often told hence it is an honour to be part of a team that works towards getting these stories out.

Is there a specific issue or cause that is close to your heart at the moment?

Education will always be a cause close to my heart because it has the power to liberate one from ignorance and poverty. It gives a certain sense of power and a chance to access opportunities in the world. Unfortunately in my home country and many other developing countries, many children face huge barriers in accessing education. For this reason, I endeavour to champion the right to access education in my country. As a regional coordinator at VOICE, I am in charge of the implementation of VOICE's outreach activities in education. VOICE supports the education of four young students in Kenya through the provision of tuition fees and school supplies. This support provides an opportunity for the children to study without having to worry, like all children should be able to.

When you were a student, were you involved in student initiatives at your university and if yes, what did you learn back then?

Yes, I was very much involved in student initiatives. I was active in sports and student associations. Through these initiatives, I learned a lot of values that continue to shape my perspective on life today. I learned the value of working in a team, the importance of giving back and most of the experiences inspired my interest in international development.

What are your thoughts on the way women in Africa are portrayed in Western discourses?

Women from Africa are often portrayed as victims who lack agency in their own lives. In my opinion, this is far from the truth. While women in Africa face numerous challenges such as poverty and oppression from systemic patriarchal norms, most of the women are far from being the weak victims in need of saving. On the contrary, women in African countries are the most resilient individuals, who fight every day to make their lives and those of their families better. More discourses in the west need to put more effort into portraying a more balanced story and give credit to the efforts that these women make in their day-to-day lives to improve their livelihoods.

Many experts postulate that some combination of institutionalized legal discrimination, cultural practices, lack of education and religious beliefs about women contribute to gender inequality in the MENA region and in Africa. In what ways can women's rights be advanced to ensure gender equality?

There are various efforts that are currently underway in advancing women's rights to achieve gender equality. In my opinion, advancing women's rights is not a singular process but ought to happen as a series of efforts. For instance, in many African contexts, for real and long-lasting impact to be achieved in achieving gender equality, men have to be part of the conversation. I believe when men understand the value of empowering women in their societies, then they will be even greater champions of gender equality. This is not an easy task as it calls for challenging cultural and societal norms which often favour men and view women as secondary. However, it needs to be done. One of the places to begin for instance would be in our homes, where the deconstruction of norms that impede progress towards gender equality can take place.

Sheila, what in your opinion are the most important barriers to entry that prevent access to higher education in your home country and in Africa generally?

One of the main barriers to access to higher education is lack of financing/poverty. While there were efforts by the government in my home country to subsidize higher education in the past, some students still face huge challenges in raising funds to go to school. The government has made some efforts by providing accessible student loans to students who are economically challenged, however, not all students are able to raise the difference that is required. The problem of financing can be seen across the continent where we have had student led movements such as the fees must fall movement in South Africa, calling for a decrease in the cost of higher education.

The Power of Multiple Stories: A postscript from our writing advisor

Catherine Banner

When the first VOICE anthology, *A Definition of Snow*, was published, I was asked to contribute a brief postscript to the book. At the time, I was unsure if there was anything I could add t o what the writers had already said. I had worked with some of them for years, over multiple drafts, and I felt I knew them well. But how to describe that intense and humbling experience, that long work of collaboration and excavation? And besides, my place as writing advisor had always been behind the scenes, not a speaking role in the project but a listening one.

So in the end, I decided to describe that experience of listening. At the time, I wanted to express what it had been like to be one of the first readers of the book, and to support the writers to put their stories so powerfully onto the page. And I wanted to describe what seemed to me so crucial and important about those stories, as a reader. At the time, I drew on the words of another more eloquent writer, Chimamanda Ngozi Adichie, to try to frame the urgent problem that the first VOICE book had managed to address.

Stories possess a great power, I wrote, *to connect us, to challenge us, to open up experiences of other worlds and other lives. As humans, we are storytelling creatures. We can't listen to another person's story and fail to become involved. To listen to another person's story, on some level, is to understand them. For this reason, many writers and readers believe that stories can be a force for good. But there is another, more problematic, side to storytelling. Sometimes the very power of stories, the strength of their message, can get in the way of truth. Sometimes stories can be a force for deception. What happens when a story, instead of containing a powerful insight, contains a powerful stereotype? The writer Chimamanda Ngozi Adichie has spoken of "the danger of a single story".* What happens when some stories are heard, and other stories remain unread?

Because, as readers and writers know, stories are not always a force for good. Often, they are used to suppress the facts, to spread harmful narratives, to manipulate, to obfuscate. Indeed, in 'Western' countries, no matter how many books are published or how many newspapers printed, the selection of stories available to us, especially from and about those places that we perceive as distant from us, still often seems dangerously distorted and incomplete. In the manner of an imperialist's map, some terrain – that which is familiar or privileged – has endlessly been drawn and redrawn, while other parts of the map have been sketchily filled in, by cartographers who don't know the landscape, or think they know it, or are hostile to it, or have already coloured it over with preconceived ideas, or only notice those particular caricatures which confirm their prejudice.

And yet, as storytelling creatures, our perception of the reality and humanity of others is powerfully affected by our ability to imagine their lives and worlds. In the absence of a full story, we often fall back on a simplistic narrative. That is the kind of single story that I think Chimamanda Ngozi Adichie was so worried about. And it was this kind of single story that VOICE, from the beginning, set out to challenge.

One solution to the danger of simplistic or harmful narratives has always been to create spaces where multiple voices – voices that have previously been ignored or silenced – can be heard. VOICE is one such rare and crucial space. I feel I have the privilege to re-enter it each time I read the writers' words. In that space, the problematic single story surrounding international development is challenged and counterbalanced by a multiplicity of powerful and thought-provoking narratives. Instead of one story, with one message, I find myself encountering multiple individual voices, which are meaningful, moving, nuanced and full of complexity. I am certain that listening to such voices can be transformative. Indeed, since 2019, when the first VOICE anthology was published, many other readers have got in touch to describe the profound difference in their perceptions that came about after encountering the stories in the book.

But VOICE has had another powerful effect, too, perhaps the most important – and one that I did not foresee. After the first book was published, I was surprised and moved by the thoughts that many of the writers shared with us about the experience of putting their stories into words. Indeed, these thoughts are eloquently summed up in the 'Notes from a VOICE Writer' by Golda Poni which is included at the start of this book. 'There is power in your voice,' she writes. 'Your voice reveals the unseen and is the foundation for the confidence, freedom, hope, and future of those you serve. So don't hide your voice because it most likely is someone's breakthrough, transformation, and future.' Many of the VOICE writers echoed these same ideas. The act of raising their voices had energized and empowered them to return with a new sense of purpose to their work and examine it afresh. The act of speaking, and not just the act of listening, it turned out, could be revolutionary.

Two years later, *Shifting Lines* represents a vital space for the continuation of that dialogue, where VOICE writers can be heard and VOICE readers can listen. It also represents a crucial widening. The new writers in this book return to many topics of concern to the first writers – global warming, gender inequalities, social enterprise, civil war, activism. But they also widen the dialogue in important ways, with new emphases like entrepreneurship, technology and community organizing. Their stories speak for themselves. The writers raise their voices with power and eloquence. They have a great deal to add to our map of the world. They do so while remaining completely themselves, irreducible and unique.

Catherine Banner is the writing advisor for VOICE, and works with all the writers to support them while developing their stories, as well as helping to prepare Shifting Lines *for publication.*

A Note about Project VOICE

Project VOICE, *Voices of Individuals Conveying Experiences*, was founded in February 2016 with the aim of projecting voices which might not otherwise reach readers: the voices of individuals working for change in their own communities. Since then, VOICE has been working to collect the stories of people from all over the world who work or volunteer in social, humanitarian, development or peace-related fields in their home country or region. Our team currently has eleven dedicated members from six different countries of origin, speaking ten different languages. Our writers work with our head, regional coordinators, writing advisor and, where necessary, translators, to develop their stories. In 2019, VOICE published *A Definition of Snow*, an anthology of fourteen stories by VOICE writers. *Shifting Lines* is the second book published by VOICE.

Our publications build on our seven principles of fairness, diversity, respect, tolerance, independence, engagement and non-profitability, which form the basis of anything we do. Working with our writers to help them tell their stories has been the core of our work in the past three years, but VOICE takes its mission to project voices further.

At VOICE, we have seen first-hand how exchanging stories can overcome divisions and be a force for positive change in the world. Through our Connect Outreach programme, we build bridges between our writers or other individuals dedicating their lives to affecting change in their home countries or region, and our audiences. Through events, workshops, partnership groups and discussion groups, we enable a direct exchange and dialogue between individuals and groups across borders, cultures and languages, based on a shared interest or simply curiosity. We closely liaise with our local contacts to make sure the exchange is as fruitful as possible, and to actively bridge cultural gaps. At the same time, we aim to allow Connect Outreach participants to build individual relationships and communicate directly and openly with their Connect contacts. Connect is open to everyone – whether for long-term dialogue or one-off events.

VOICE is also active in two Outreach projects in Kenya and Tanzania. In Kenya, we currently sponsor four young minds in finding their voices by covering their school fees and all school expenses. In Tanzania, VOICE supports local women and girls' projects with our partner, SASA Foundation, helping beneficiaries build their story and get heard locally.

In 2019, VOICE became a registered non-profit association in Germany (e.V. mit Gemeinnützigkeit). If you would like to get involved directly or learn more about Outreach options, VOICE is always looking for dedicated team members all over the world. To find out more about the book, how we work, and the projects we do, visit our website at www.projectingvoices.org or get in touch directly at info@projectingvoices.org.

The VOICE Writers[10]

Akinyi Awora (Kenya)
Akinyi prides herself on having growth as a core value. This is the driving force behind her commitment towards continuous improvement in development solutions. A relentless advocate for equality, her life's work is dedicated to designing solutions that disrupt the way the world thinks about development. She has worked as a design thinking consultant helping businesses, civil society organizations and public servants design products and programmes built for impact. She is a Mandela Washington Fellow, an Ashoka Young Changemaker, a One Young World Enterprise for Peace Ambassador, an Africa Youth for SDGs Champion and a relentless force in advocating for gender-responsive approaches to sustainable development. Her work with

[10] In alphabetical order of first name.

communities in driving economic development earned her the Women of Heart Golden Award from the Women of Heart Foundation in London, UK. Her work has been featured on global platforms such as the Acumen Fund and World Connect. She currently works and lives in Siaya County, rural western Kenya.

Aravinth Panch (Sri Lanka)

Aravinth is a social entrepreneur empowering underserved communities in war-affected regions of Sri Lanka. He was born at a difficult time when his family lost several members as collateral damages to the civil war. At 14, he escaped the country in fear of becoming a child soldier; he was exiled as a young refugee for ten years and returned when the war ended. His craving to support those who went through the same life experiences propelled him to co-found DreamSpace Academy – a non-profit social enterprise tackling local socio-economic and environmental challenges through challenge-based learning, grassroots innovation and impact venture building.

Jhanisse Vaca Daza (Bolivia)

Jhanisse Vaca Daza is co-founder of Ríos de Pie, a citizen nonviolence movement focused on human rights and environmental rights in Bolivia. She is also Network Manager at the Human Rights Foundation. Jhanisse began teaching nonviolence in Bolivia at the age of 23, which later led to the creation of the youth nonviolence movement Ríos de Pie (Standing Rivers in English). Standing Rivers played a key role driving humanitarian efforts during the Amazon fires crisis in 2019 and the COVID-19 crisis in Bolivia. They have educated thousands of Bolivians in nonviolent resistance and continue to do humanitarian work today. Jhanisse obtained her honours bachelor's degree at Kent State University, where she studied International Relations thanks to scholarships. She subsequently completed the Nonviolent Movement Leadership for Social Progress online programme at Harvard Kennedy School. Her previous work experience includes work in programme AVISA, which protects child victims of sexual abuse in Santa Cruz, Bolivia; legal assistant in defence of undocumented immigrants in The Shagin Law Group LLC (USA); and consultation for NGOs on nonviolence work in Bolivia.

Jonathan Chu (Malaysia)

Jonathan Chu is the Director of 95% The Business Culture Consultants, a consultancy company that aims to turn workplaces into Joyplaces. He believes that a workplace can truly be a Joyplace when people are not only results-oriented, but people-conscious. That guides him as he consults, facilitates, designs and implements culture transformation programmes. With his entrepreneurial and coaching experience, he also consults and guides start-ups and social enterprises in business modelling, marketing, and sales. In the spirit of giving back, he functions as the Coordinating Ambassador for One Young World and works hard at building the community in Southeast Asia. He is now in the process of establishing two more start-ups – one in FinTech and another in EdTech, and aims to continually build strong organizations and teams.

José Zea and Laura Velásquez (Colombia)

José is a self-taught programmer. He has worked with start-ups since age 16. José was named Top Canadian Researcher by the Bombardier Fellowship 2018-2019, and one of Colombia's top 20 under 21 young innovators by the Disney Foundation and Ashoka. He dropped out of school for a year to build a net-zero house for the future in Latam, raising US$80,000 from the US Department of Energy for the construction. José is the CEO and co-founder at Arkangel AI, where he builds AI algorithms for early detection of diseases.

Laura is the president and co-founder of Arkangel AI, a technology company that uses artificial intelligence to attempt to end the crisis of highly preventable diseases through early detection of diseases and so reduce inequality in access to health in the Global South. Laura is passionate about entrepreneurship and is committed to solving global problems with the use of artificial intelligence. She has previous experience in international contexts, such as New York City, Bogota, Santiago de Chile, Madrid, and Montreal, supporting large high-growth and high-impact start-ups. That has allowed her to develop the ability to create strategies for growth, digital transformation, and impact globally. She has been the only woman and the only Latina to win in the history of the Global Everis Awards. She is a "Dream Maker" and believes in innovation as the primary weapon of change.

Jovita S. Mlay (Tanzania)

Jovita is the Executive Director of SASA Foundation. SASA Foundation aims to enhance productive capacity and inclusion of women, children and other marginalized groups into socio-economic systems and structures from family and community to national levels to contribute towards economic growth and poverty reduction in Tanzania. Jovita is happily married and a mother of three children. Jovita holds a bachelor's degree in Commerce and Accounting, and a master's degree in International Trade, both from the University of Dar es Salaam, Tanzania.

Marjorie Atuhurra (Uganda)

Atuhurra Angella Marjorie is a Ugandan social entrepreneur and the founder of the Gejja Women Foundation in Mpigi, Uganda. She is an energetic, ambitious woman who has developed a mature and responsible approach to the task of female empowerment in her community. She is passionate about girls and women, the environment and how best we can eradicate poverty, reduce unemployment and shift into a more sustainable globe starting with her herself, her community and her environment.

Mercy Adong (Uganda)

Mercy comes from a poor family in northern Uganda and is 29 years old. Most of her youth there was civil war and she lived in a refugee camp for several years. She could not follow her dream of studying medicine but became a nursery teacher. Later she taught at schools in refugee camps in South Sudan and Uganda. She loves people and especially children. Presently, she is trying to become self-employed as a small-scale entrepreneur. She is a cheerful person who loves life, enjoying beautiful clothes and music. Religion is important for her. She is a single mother of a wonderful four-year-old daughter.

Prakriti Bhandari (Nepal)

Prakriti is a founding member and Secretary of the Executive Board of Shangri-La Development Association. Shangri-La Development Association aims to improve the lives of people through health, education, participation, capacity building and opportunity enlargement programmes. The association's vision is to pioneer a prosperous Nepal and a harmonious world by creating critical, honest, and harmonious development-oriented world citizens who aim to create an equitable peaceful and prosperous society. They aim to do this by including and consulting with the excluded and disadvantaged peoples in the development process. Prakriti grew up in Shangri-La Orphanage Home from the age of six. She holds a bachelor's degree in Law and Business Management from the Kathmandu University School of Law.

Wendi Njeri (Kenya)

Wendi Njeri is 16 years old and currently in the final year of high school. Wendi is the founder of Books in Baskets Mini-libraries, a Library Project whose vision is to provide books to school-going children who have no or limited access to a library. She has officially launched two mini-libraries. Wendi hopes to develop and support the African continent by enriching the education system, making opportunities available to reduce inequalities. Wendi believes that education should not be a trap but a building block to something greater. Wendi's hobbies include reading, baking, cooking and researching. The reading and research interests have given Wendi a broad perspective on topical issues and the world at large.

The VOICE Team

VOICE is incredibly diverse: we connect with VOICE writers from all over the world, and work in four official languages. This would not be possible without our team dedicating their free time to the project. Our team comes from six different countries and speaks a total of ten different languages.

Annina Lux – VOICE Founder, Head (Executive Committee) and Editor

Annina is the founder and head of VOICE. She is the editor of *Shifting Lines*. Annina was born in 1992 in Germany. She has lived and worked in various countries, including the UK, France, the US and Bolivia, where she worked in a rural hospital. She holds a BA in History from the University of Durham, UK, and an MA in International Security from the Paris School of International Affairs (Sciences Po). Her experience in Bolivia led her to establish VOICE in 2016. Annina currently lives and works in Berlin.

Florian Wintermeyer – Secretary (Executive Committee) and Translator (German and French)

Florian is VOICE's Secretary in our Executive Committee and works as a German and French translator for VOICE. He holds a double master's from the Paris School of International Affairs (Sciences Po) and Freie Universität Berlin. Having lived and studied in many different countries, he now lives and works in New York.

Jonas Lux – Finance Officer (Executive Committee) and Graphic Support

Jonas is VOICE's finance officer in the Executive Committee. He also provides graphic design support for the VOICE website, events and publications. Jonas has lived in Germany and New Zealand. He is currently enrolled at the University of Augsburg.

Catherine Banner – Writing Advisor

Catherine's role is as writing advisor to VOICE. She is a writer born in the UK and living in Turin, Italy. She studied at Fitzwilliam College, Cambridge, and has previously worked as a teacher of English and literacy. With an interest in human rights and education, she is a member of PEN International Writers' Circle, and works as a volunteer tutor at the *Arsenale della Piazza* social project. Her work is published by Penguin Random House and has been translated into 24 languages.

Sheila Chepkoech – Regional Contact for Africa and Translator (Swahili)

Sheila is VOICE's Regional Contact for Africa and also a contributing VOICE writer in *A Definition of Snow*. She is a Kenyan national working in the field of development studies. She has a bachelor's degree in International Relations from the United States International University of Africa and a master's degree in International Development from the Paris School of International Affairs (Sciences Po). She currently lives in Eldoret, Kenya.

Bárbara del Bosque Salmerón – Regional Contact for Latin America and Translator (Spanish)

Bárbara works for VOICE as Regional Contact for Central and South America and as a Spanish translator. She also shared her experience in *A Definition of Snow*. She was born in Orizaba, México, in 1992, and has a bachelor's degree in Nutrition and Food Science. She has been involved in talks and workshops about healthy eating and nutrition in different towns and communities in México, Brazil and Paraguay, where she worked as a volunteer in educational projects. She currently works as a nutritionist in both a governmental hospital and a private practice and also works as a volunteer Emergency Medical Technician in Orizaba, Vera Cruz.

Margot Ossola – Outreach Coordinator and Translator (French and Italian)

Margot leads our Outreach Germany initiative and works as a French and Italian translator for VOICE. She is a master's student at the Hertie School in Berlin, where she currently lives. She was born in Italy and is half French half Italian. In 2020 she joined the VOICE project because she wanted to contribute to the collection and the projection of the voices of authors worldwide. Additionally, she wanted to be part of the diverse VOICE team while dedicating her time and skills to a meaningful cause.

Alena Gold – Media and Communications Manager

Alena is responsible for the communication and the media management of VOICE. She has a bachelor's degree in

European Studies from the Technical University of Chemnitz and studied for a semester at the University of Santiago de Compostela. She also has a Media and Communications master's from the University of Applied Sciences Mittweida. She currently lives in Jena, Germany, where she works as a science communicator.

Alexander Punter – Technology and Web Master
Alex joined VOICE in order to provide technical support and website maintenance. He is a British science graduate of the University of Durham. He also holds a chemistry doctorate from the University of Marseille. He currently lives in the UK.

Jan-Frederik Westedt – Social Media Coordinator
Jan joined VOICE in 2021 and is responsible for our Social Media channels. He also supports our Outreach in Germany. Originally, Jan comes from Hamburg, Germany. He is currently studying Media & Communication Management at Macromedia University in Berlin, which has become his second home.

Philina Tempelmeier – Writing Team
Philina supports our VOICE writing team. She was born in 1993 and grew up in Germany. She lived in the UK for five years, where she finished school and graduated from Durham University with a BA in Economics and International Relations. Philina currently studies law at the Ludwig-Maximilians-University in Munich.

A Thank You from the Editor

Annina Lux

In the preface, I said that the process of finding our writers is easy, because they stand out. What I did not capture is how thrilling it is to meet these inspiring individuals, and what a privilege it is to work with them. On top of standing up, speaking up, reaching out, asking questions or moving when the majority of people are doing the opposite, they also took the time and effort to share their story with VOICE and with our readers, whether in our publications or in outreach events. A massive thank you to all of our VOICE writers. You are simply incredible.

The same holds true for the amazing VOICE team. The process of shifting lines is inherently complex, and we could not wish for a better team of people to work with on this. To write down everything I am grateful for to each individual one of you would require its own book, so here is a short version: A massive, massive thank you to (in order of appearance):

… Sheila for your strikingly sensitive way of leading our Kenya Outreach. The way you handle the administrative and personal complexities of coordinating our local projects and your support as a regional contact is simply remarkable. Your positivity and confidence in what we do is so refreshing.

… Alena for your persistent support, your incredible positive energy and your extremely skilful way of making me think about telling our own story as VOICE. Your calm yet passionate and pragmatic way of handling anything that comes our way has been unbelievably energizing.

... Alex for your extraordinary way of structuring our (finance) processes and, the quiet and powerful way in which you centre our team, and for always, always being there when you are needed, on the shortest of notice and at any point, day or night.

... Philina for your extremely thoughtful work as internal reader kick-starting *Shifting Lines'* very first stories, your incredible flexibility for their short turnarounds and your constant support over the years.

... Bárbara for your absolutely energizing way of working and supporting VOICE. Your ability to carry the whole team with your wonderful spirit, whether in person or digitally, is astounding.

...Jonas for your extremely intelligent way of juggling the various financial bureaucracies behind VOICE to the highest transparency and accountability standards, enabling the next generation of VOICE writers. And yet again for putting us on the map, literally. Your dedication to building bridges and making even the smallest things work is amazing.

... Margot for not just managing to join VOICE at a time we were going full speed, but to accelerate our Outreach in Germany in such an incredible way. Your perseverance and reliability under the highest pressure in heading Outreach Germany and supporting Communications is astounding.

… Jan-Frederik for supporting us extremely diligently where and when we needed it most, and for being so incredibly passionate about VOICE from the second you joined the team.

Two VOICE team members deserve some very special thank yous for this book:

Florian, because without you, Projecting Voices e.V. would literally not exist. Thank you for your unwavering dedication to giving VOICE an official administrative home. Thank you for going not one but so many extra miles to make VOICE what it is today, foreseeing every pitfall and mastering all of them so incredibly skillfully. And most of all, thank you for having my back at every single turn in the past two years, making this book possible. Your unconditional support and drive for anything VOICE has carried the team so far in the past two years. I have no idea what I would have done without you. Thank you.

Catherine, for diving into *Shifting Lines* head-first and without hesitation the second I asked for your help in editing. Thank you for the amazing way in which you completely avoid intruding in any of our writers´ stories, but are still present in every single one of them to me in a beautiful, invisible second layer of background conversations. It is the conversations with you that turned *Shifting Lines* from a manuscript into a book. You have no idea how grateful I am for having you as a sparring partner and writing advisor in the VOICE writing team.

Without all of you, *Shifting Lines* would not have been possible.

To me, every book also tells a story that is not captured in its lines. The entire VOICE team and I are immensely thankful to all those who supported and accompanied us on the way to *Shifting Lines*. Thank you to Anna Werner for your excitement and energy in bringing VOICE to the next level and starting off *Shifting Lines*. To Julia Hill and Cecilie Gronningsaeter for your extremely helpful thoughts on the book as its very first external readers. To Niamh Hatton for your careful and sensitive editing and proofreading, which added so much to the quality of the final text. To the Soroptimist International Chapter Ingolstadt, for your continuing support of VOICE and our publications over the years. To Jens-Peter Labus and Grit Reiche with Marike, Emily, Paula and Elisa for your support of our Tanzania and Kenya projects, enabling future change-makers to find their voices. To Wolfgang and Petra Lux as well as Helga and Siegfried Wirth for helping the next generation of VOICE writers in Kenya kick-start their stories. And last but not least, thank you to all our incredible readers and supporters – your dedication to all of our VOICE projects, your moving messages on our books and the many thought-provoking conversations we have had over the years continue to prove to us just how far all of us can shift lines together. A massive thank you to all of you.

A DEFINITION OF SNOW
FOURTEEN VOICES OF SOCIAL, HUMANITARIAN, DEVELOPMENT AND PEACE WORKERS WORKING IN THEIR NATIVE COUNTRY OR REGION
ANNINA LUX (EDITOR)

What if 14 individuals, working for change in their own communities around the world, came together to tell their stories? In *A Definition of Snow*, 14 writers do just that. Gathered by Project VOICE over a period of three years, the writers describe their day-to-day experiences working in social, humanitarian, medical, development and peace-related fields, in Africa, Latin America, Asia and the Middle East, in ways that are powerful, honest and thought-provoking. Such stories, until now, have been mostly unavailable. But they are highly important – and they should be told by those who experienced them and continue to experience them on a daily basis. *A Definition of Snow* aims to project these unique voices, and bring their stories to readers for the first time.

I come from Africa, a continent that is very rich in many ways. We are very wealthy in non-material things such as happiness, laughter, joy, contentment, generosity and love. We are also wealthy in natural resources, breath-taking scenery and fertile land. However, we are famously known in the Western world for poverty, disease, corruption and war. The truth is, we are more than that and there is our side of the story that is often not told.

- Sheila Chepkoech, Kenya

I wanted to be free of dictatorship. I wanted to be able to speak my mind without being punished. I wanted to decide for myself what I wanted to be in life. Nobody should decide for me.

- Hintsa Solomon, Eritrea/Germany

Girls no longer marry at 14, they do not stop school at 14 – this is probably one of the best things we have done for the community. It is not easy to change people's mentality and their convictions.

- Noha Rbeiz, Lebanon

ISBN 978-3-7549-0553-1
9 783754 905531 00003
www.epubli.de